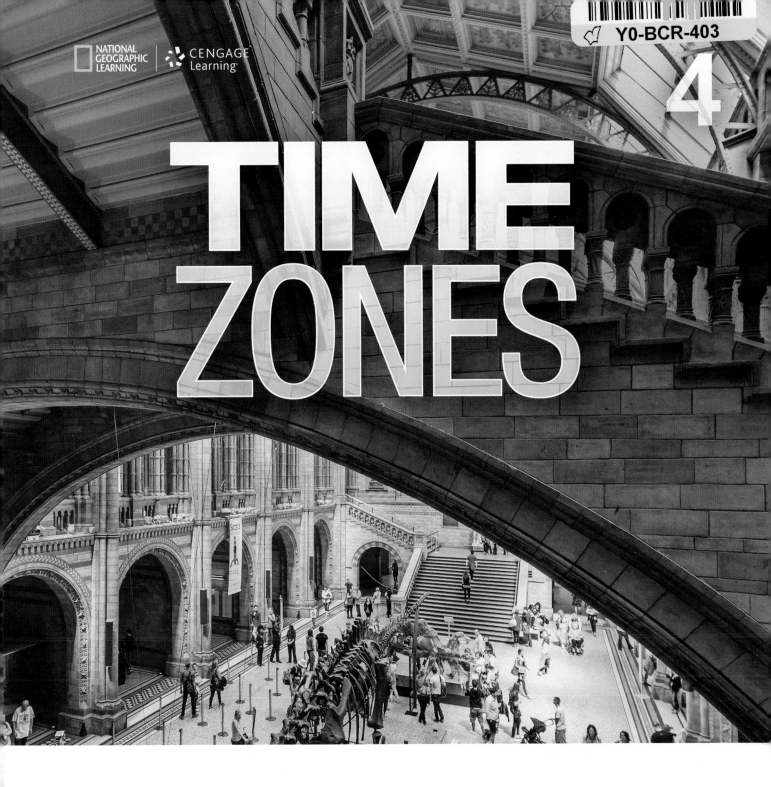

NATIONAL GEOGRAPHIC LEARNING

CENGAGE Learning

4

TIME ZONES

David Bohlke
Jennifer Wilkin

SECOND EDITION

NATIONAL GEOGRAPHIC LEARNING | CENGAGE Learning

Australia • Brazil • Japan • Korea • Mexico • Singapore • Spain • United Kingdom • United States

Time Zones Student Book 4
Second Edition

David Bohlke and Jennifer Wilkin

Publisher: Andrew Robinson

Senior Development Editor: Derek Mackrell

Development Editors: Sian Mavor,
Charlotte Sharman

Assistant Editor: Melissa Pang

Director of Global Marketing: Ian Martin

Product Marketing Manager: Anders Bylund

Media Researcher: Leila Hishmeh

Senior Director of Production:
Michael Burggren

Senior Content Project Manager:
Tan Jin Hock

Manufacturing Planner:
Mary Beth Hennebury

Compositor: Cenveo Publisher Services

Cover/Text Design: Creative Director:
Christopher Roy, Art Director: Scott Baker,
Senior Designer: Michael Rosenquest

Cover Photo: Natural History Museum,
London, England: Massimo Borchi/Atlantide
Phototravel/Corbis

Student Book with Online Workbook:
ISBN-13: 978-1-305-51074-6

Student Book:
ISBN-13: 978-1-305-25987-4

National Geographic Learning
20 Channel Center Street
Boston, MA 02210
USA

Cengage Learning is a leading provider of customized learning solutions with employees residing in nearly 40 different countries and sales in more than 125 countries around the world. Find your local representative at:
www.cengage.com

Cengage Learning products are represented in Canada by Nelson Education, Ltd.

Visit National Geographic Learning online at **NGL.Cengage.com**

Visit our corporate website at **www.cengage.com**

Printed in China
Print Number: 06   Print Year: 2018

Contents

SCOPE AND SEQUENCE

Unit	Functions	Grammar	Vocabulary	Pronunciation	Read, Write, & Watch
Page 6 **1** **I Love Making Jewelry!**	Talking about hobbies and interests **Real English:** *Tell me about it!*	**Gerunds:** *She likes watching movies.* *I enjoy cooking.* *Does he like doing puzzles?*	Hobbies Interests	Intonation in statements, questions, exclamations	**Reading:** By the Numbers **Writing:** Description **Video:** Robot Games
Page 16 **2** **How Long Have You Been Playing Cricket?**	Identifying different sports Describing one's sports activities **Real English:** *Give it a try.*	**Present perfect progressive:** *She's been working hard.* *I've been playing badminton.* **Adverbs of time:** *lately* *recently* *since* *for*	Sports	Weak form of *been*	**Reading:** North American Odyssey **Writing:** Biography **Video:** Life Rolls On
Page 26 **3** **You Could Ask for Advice.**	Asking for and giving advice **Real English:** *You know . . .*	**Modals:** *should, could, would* **Verbs with *try*:** *try telling, try asking* **Other expressions for giving advice:** *Why don't you . . .* *If I were you . . .*	Problems and advice	Weak forms of *should* and *could*	**Reading:** Vision of Hope **Writing:** Letter **Video:** Eco-Fuel Africa
Page 36 **4** **The Koala Was Taken to a Shelter.**	Talking about animal rescue **Real English:** *It's up to you.*	**Passive voice without an agent:** *An injured animal was brought into the shelter yesterday.* *The cats were checked for any injuries.* *Is an injured animal given medicine?*	Wild animals Animal rescue	Intonation in a series	**Reading:** Bear Rescue **Writing:** News article **Video:** Animal Portraits
Page 46 **5** **How Was It Formed?**	Describing the formation of natural landscapes **Real English:** *There it is.*	**Passive voice with an agent:** *Valleys are formed by glaciers.* *The beach is being washed away by the sea.* *The rock was broken apart by ice.*	Natural formations Phrasal verbs	Contrastive stress	**Reading:** Cave of Secrets **Writing:** Tourist guide **Video:** Mountain River Cave
Page 56 **6** **Look at That Narwhal!**	Talking about the importance of conserving marine animals and their habitats **Real English:** *You're telling me . . .*	**Non-restrictive relative clauses:** *The narwhal, which is a type of whale, has a long, straight tusk.* *My uncle, who visits every summer, is a marine biologist.*	Marine animals	Relative clauses	**Reading:** Cities in the Sea **Writing:** Formal letter **Video:** Saving Our Reefs

I LOVE MAKING
JEWELRY!

Many people find making jewelry a creative and fun hobby.

Preview

A 1-01 **Listen to the conversations.** Match the people (Jeff, Maria, Zac, and Wendy) to their hobbies. Write **J**, **M**, **Z**, or **W**.

making jewelry _____

building models _____

writing a blog _____

baking _____

B 1-01 **Listen again.** Complete the chart.

	WHEN	WHERE
Jeff	on Wednesdays	
Maria	on the weekends	
Zac		in the school cafeteria
Wendy		at her aunt's place

C **Talk with a partner.** Do you have any hobbies? What do you like doing?

I like reading comic books.

How many comics do you have?

I only have about 30, but I've read over 200!

Language Focus

A 🎧1–02 **Listen and read.** Then repeat the conversation and replace the words in blue.

REAL ENGLISH Tell me about it!

B **Practice with a partner.** Replace any words to make your own conversation.

🎧1–03

TALKING ABOUT HOBBIES AND INTERESTS		
She He	**likes / loves**	**watching movies.** **playing the drums.** **cooking.** **jogging.**
I They	**enjoy / don't like**	
Does he **like doing** puzzles?		Yes, he **does.**
Do you **like skiing**?		No, **I can't stand it.** **I don't mind it.**

C 🎧 1-04 **Complete the conversation.** Use the correct forms of the words. Then listen and check your answers.

> hike   perform   play   join   stay

Kara: Hey, Paulo, have you signed up for any after-school activities yet?

Paulo: No, not yet. I love singing, so I might look into (1) _____ the musical theater club.

Kara: That would be fun! You like acting, and you're a good singer.

Paulo: Thanks. The problem is I'm not a good dancer. I'm always stepping on other people's toes. Hey! Maybe you should try out. You like (2) _____ the guitar.

Kara: Me? No, thanks. (3) _____ in front of people makes me nervous.

Paulo: Well, there's the yoga club.

Kara: No way! I can't stand yoga. Plus, (4) _____ inside even longer after school doesn't sound like fun!

Paulo: So why don't you join an outdoors club? Do you like (5) _____ ?

Kara: That's a great idea! I love the outdoors.

D 🎧 1-05 **Listen to the conversation.** What does each person think of the activities below? Write ☺, ☺, or ☹.

	LUCIA	WES
baking		
swimming		
singing		
playing video games		

E **Talk with a partner.** Look at the activities in **D**. Do you like those activities? Why or why not?

> I like singing. It makes me feel relaxed.

The Real World

Extreme Collectors

Hobbies can be big business.
Americans spend about $75 billion on their hobbies each year. Some people enjoy collecting things as a hobby, and they sometimes spend a lot of time and money on it.

A 🎧1-06 **Listen.** Circle **T** for True or **F** for False.

1. Dave shares videos of his collection online.	T	F
2. Dave's wife wants him to buy fewer action figures.	T	F
3. Alex collects cards of different baseball players.	T	F
4. Dave and Alex are spending less time and money on their hobbies now.	T	F

B 🎧1-06 **Listen again.** Complete the chart.

	SIZE OF COLLECTION	VALUE OF COLLECTION	TIME SPENT ON HOBBY
Dave			
Alex			

CRITICAL THINKING Do you like collecting things? Do you think extreme collecting is a problem for Dave or Alex? Why or why not?

Pronunciation

Intonation in statements, questions, exclamations

A 🎧1-07 **Listen and repeat.**

1. He hates singing.

2. He hates singing?

3. He hates singing!

B 🎧1-08 **Listen.** Complete the sentences with a period (**.**), question mark (**?**), or exclamation mark (**!**).

1. Antonio loves playing video games ____

2. Fred hates doing word puzzles ____

3. Sarah doesn't mind doing the dishes ____

4. Peter can't stand shopping ____

5. Yun likes baking ____

C **Work with a partner.** Take turns to read the sentences in **B**.

DO YOU KNOW?

People in ____ spend the most amount of time on leisure activities.

a. the United States
b. Spain
c. New Zealand

Communication

Do a survey. Complete the sentences with information that is true for you. Then interview three other students. Ask follow-up questions. Write their names and responses.

NAMES			
I like playing _____.			
I enjoy hanging out at _____.			
I love watching _____.			
I don't mind helping out with _____ at home.			
I don't like playing _____.			
I love _____ on weekends.			
I enjoy listening to _____.			

Do you like playing tennis?

Yes, I do.

Oh, me, too! How often do you play?

Reading

A **Look at the charts.** Check (✓) the information about teens that is shown.

◯ club involvement   ◯ time spent reading   ◯ changing trends in leisure time

B **Skim the article.** Choose the most suitable heading for each section.

> a. More Friends, but More Alone Time   b. Effects of Technology   c. Remaining Active

1 ___   **2** ___   **3** ___

C **Talk with a partner.** How much time each day do you spend using a computer or other electronic devices for leisure?

BY THE NUMBERS

🎧1–09

Teenagers in the United States—like teens in many countries—have more leisure time today than ever before. But over a number of decades, there have been some changes in how teenagers spend their time after school.

1 Participating in school clubs remains a common after-school activity. According to a study, the three most popular types are sports clubs, performing arts clubs, and academic clubs—the same as 20 years ago. While overall participation in these clubs has gradually dropped over the last two decades, this does not mean that students are less active.

Teens today are more likely to volunteer or work with neighborhood or community groups. High school seniors are thinking about college. They want a competitive college application that includes a variety of experiences. They know that academic grades, school activities, and community involvement are all important when applying to college.

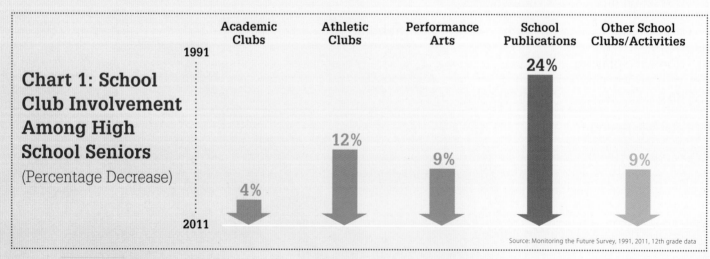

Chart 1: School Club Involvement Among High School Seniors
(Percentage Decrease)

	Academic Clubs	Athletic Clubs	Performance Arts	School Publications	Other School Clubs/Activities
1991 → 2011	4%	12%	9%	24%	9%

Source: Monitoring the Future Survey, 1991, 2011, 12th grade data

2 While the kinds of activities that students participate in at school have not changed greatly, high school teens now spend their leisure time out of school in very different ways. For example, teens today are less likely to visit a friend in person than 20 years ago. And—perhaps unsurprisingly—they are far less likely to read a print newspaper or magazine.

One of the reasons for these changes is access to technology. Teens today have greater access to the Internet, and it has increasingly become their main channel for socializing and getting information.

Calling and texting are the most popular modes of communication among teens. Teens also connect with friends online through social media. 92% of American teens go online every day. 71% use more than one social networking site, with Facebook and Instagram being the most popular platforms. A study in 2011 showed that 29% of teens talked to friends every day through social networking sites. This trend is likely to continue; between 2006 and 2011, messaging through social media increased from 21% to 29%.

Chart 2: Most Popular Social Media Platforms

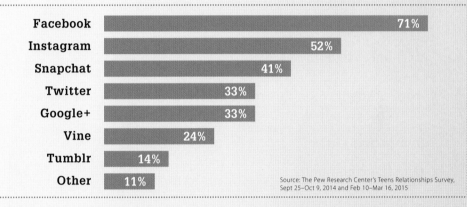

Facebook	71%
Instagram	52%
Snapchat	41%
Twitter	33%
Google+	33%
Vine	24%
Tumblr	14%
Other	11%

Source: The Pew Research Center's Teens Relationships Survey, Sept 25–Oct 9, 2014 and Feb 10–Mar 16, 2015

3 What leisure activities do teens **DO LESS TODAY THAN THREE DECADES AGO?**

The list is long:

- watching TV
- going to the movies
- meeting friends
- reading
- writing
- going to the mall
- going to friends' parties

They may have more **FRIENDS** than ever before, but they actually spend more of their time **ALONE** — these days.—

Chart 3: Changes in Leisure Time Use Among High School Seniors

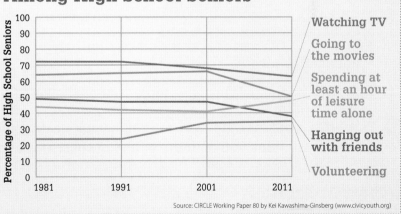

Source: CIRCLE Working Paper 80 by Kei Kawashima-Ginsberg (www.civicyouth.org)

The world of the teen has moved online, and it's likely to stay there.

Comprehension

IDIOM

The time when you are not working is also known as _____.

a. slowtime
b. backtime
c. downtime

A Answer the questions about *By the Numbers*.

1. Main Idea The article is about how teens today _____.

   a. spend their free time

   b. learn

   c. prepare for college

2. Vocabulary Having a "competitive" college application gives someone more _____ for college.

   a. advantage in applying

   b. time to apply

   c. chances to apply

3. Detail Students today are more involved in activities _____ than in the past.

   a. in school clubs

   b. in the community

   c. in the classroom

4. Detail According to the article, technology has changed the way teens today _____.

   a. speak

   b. travel

   c. connect with friends

5. Inference The advantage of online communication is that it allows people to _____.

   a. visit friends

   b. understand each other better

   c. interact with more people

B Complete the sentences. Use information from the charts in the article.

1. Participation in _____ showed the greatest decrease between 1991 and 2011.

2. About _____ more teenagers use Snapchat compared to Twitter and Google+.

3. In _____, the percentage of high school seniors going to the movies decreased to about 50%.

4. In 2011, about _____ more teens volunteered compared to 1981.

C Talk with a partner. How do you think your leisure time compares to that of an American teen? What do you think you do more or less of these days, compared to the past?

Writing

Write a description. Talk about what you like doing in your leisure time.

After school, I'm usually very busy with my club activities. I belong to the outdoor adventure club. At home, I don't really like watching TV, but I spend a lot of time surfing the Internet. I'm online about four hours a day. I like playing games online and chatting with my friends.

Robot Games

BEFORE YOU WATCH

Guess. What do you think FIRST stands for?

a. Fellowship of Intelligent Robot Sports Teams

b. For Inspiration and Recognition of Science and Technology

c. Fun International Robotics School Tournament

WHILE YOU WATCH

A **Check your answer to the Before You Watch question.**

B **Watch the video again.** Circle the correct answers.

1. FIRST was started by a famous (**sportsperson** / **inventor**).

2. Dean Kamen had the idea for FIRST after seeing how much kids enjoyed (**sports** / **robotics**).

3. Students work (**alone** / **in teams**) to build the robots.

4. The events in the competition are (**the same** / **different**) every year.

AFTER YOU WATCH

Talk with a partner. Are you interested in science and technology? Would you like to take part in this competition?

Participants at the FIRST Robotics Competition

2

HOW LONG HAVE YOU BEEN PLAYING CRICKET?

Preview

A 🎧 1–10 **Listen.** Match the people to the sports they do.

taekwondo   cricket   archery   rugby

1. Lucy has been   ○   ○ playing cricket   ○   ○ for two years.

2. Nathan has been ○   ○ doing archery   ○   ○ for a year.

3. Claudia has been ○   ○ playing rugby   ○   ○ since she was five.

4. Jay has been   ○   ○ doing taekwondo   ○   ○ since middle school.

B 🎧 1–10 **Listen again.** Match the people's sports to how long they have been doing them.

C **Talk with a partner.** Which sports in **A** have you done before? Which have you never done?

> I've never done taekwondo. Have you?

> Yes, I have. I took some lessons when I was younger.

Children playing cricket in India

Language Focus

A 🎧 1–11 **Listen and read.** Then repeat the conversation and replace the words in blue.

REAL ENGLISH Give it a try.

B **Practice with a partner.** Replace any words to make your own conversation.

1 Thanks for showing me around the gym.

No problem. I've been coming here **for months**, so I'm familiar with all the equipment.

since October
for a long time

2 This is a bench press. It's good for your **upper body**.

You've been using it for ten minutes. Can I give it a try?

arms
shoulders

3 And you'll **get really fit** using this rowing machine.

Let me try!

get a great workout
build strength

4 And here's my favorite— a chest press.

Um, Maya, I think you're **sitting on it backward**.

using it incorrectly
facing the wrong way

🎧 1–12

DESCRIBING ACTIONS THAT CONTINUE TO THE PRESENT	
Sandra looks tired. She**'s been working** hard **lately**. Nick is in great shape. He**'s been going** to the gym a lot **recently**.	
How long **have** you **been doing** taekwondo? How long **has** she **been playing** soccer?	I**'ve been doing** taekwondo **since** last year. She**'s been playing** soccer **for** five years.
What **have** you **been doing since** lunch?	I**'ve been playing** badminton.
Have they **been waiting long**?	Yes, they **have**. / No, they **haven't**.

C Rewrite the sentences.

1. John began doing karate when he was five years old. He's still doing it now.

   He _____ since he was five years old.

2. The snow started last night. It's still snowing now.

   It _____ last night.

3. May and Leslie started playing tennis two hours ago. They're still playing.

   They _____ two hours.

4. Jessica started kayaking at 3 o'clock. She hasn't stopped yet.

   She _____ .

5. The children began doing their homework three hours ago. They're still doing it.

   They _____ .

D 🎧 1–13 Circle the correct answers. Then listen and check.

1. Penny: You're really good at tennis, Max. Can you give me some lessons sometime?

   Max: Sure, but 1. (**I'm only playing** / **I've only been playing**) for a year. How long
           2. (**are you playing** / **have you been playing**)?

   Penny: 3. (**I've been taking** / **I was taking**) lessons since last month.

   Max: 4. (**I'm going** / **I've been going**) to be here tomorrow at 2 o'clock. Why don't you
           stop by then?

   Penny: Great! Thanks.

2. Kris: What 5. (**are you doing** / **were you doing**) now?

   Brian: I'm uploading some photos to my blog.

   Kris: Oh, 6. (**are you blogging** / **have you been blogging**) long?

   Brian: Not really. 7. (**I did** / **I've been doing**) it for only a month or so.

   Kris: 8. (**I had** / **I've been having**) a sports blog in high school.
           I should start it up again sometime.

E **Work with a partner.** Find out about the sports
he or she does. Then share the information with
another classmate.

> Janet likes rock climbing. She's been rock climbing for five
> years. She goes to an indoor climbing gym every weekend.

The Real World

New Sports

People have been playing sports for thousands of years. Three of the earliest sports were wrestling, athletics, and archery. Today, people continue to create new sports. These new sports have similarities to other sports, but have their own unique rules.

A footgolf player

A 🎧 1–14 **Listen.** Complete the sentences about the history of sports.

1. People in _____ played an early form of soccer.

2. Rules were created in 1863 to make soccer different from _____.

3. Unlike the modern Olympic Games, the ancient Games had participants from _____ only.

4. The ancient Games had _____ and religious importance.

B 🎧 1–15 **Listen.** Complete the chart with information about the new sports.

	PLACE STARTED	YEAR STARTED	NUMBER OF PLAYERS	SPORT(S) IT'S SIMILAR TO
Yakball				
Footgolf				

CRITICAL THINKING **Work with a partner.** Create a new sport. Choose a sport you know and make the new sport different in some ways. Then explain the rules of your sport to another pair.

Pronunciation
Weak form of *been*

A 🎧1–16 **Listen and repeat.**

1. She's been studying for three hours.
2. What have you been doing lately?

B 🎧1–17 **Listen.** Complete the sentences.

1. He's _____ tennis since 5 o'clock.
2. Have you _____ hard lately?
3. We've _____ here for 30 minutes.
4. She hasn't _____ to the gym much lately.
5. People have _____ yoga for thousands of years.

C **Work with a partner.** Take turns to read the sentences in **B**.

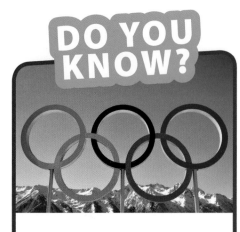

DO YOU KNOW?

What sport was no longer played in the Olympic Games after 1904, but returned in 2016?

a. golf
b. kitesurfing
c. soccer

Communication

Find someone similar to you. Complete the sentences with things that are true for you. Then find someone who has been doing the same activity. Ask an additional question.

ACTIVITIES	NAME	ADDITIONAL INFORMATION
I've been watching _____ a lot on TV.		
I've been working hard in my _____ class lately.		
I've been listening to a lot of _____ recently.		
I've been _____ since I was little.		
I've been _____ for a long time.		

I've been playing rugby since I was little. Do you play rugby?

Yes, I do.

Oh? How often do you play?

Dave and Amy Freeman traveled 18,744 kilometers across North America.

Reading

A **Look at the title.** What do you think an odyssey is?

a. a long journey full of adventure
b. a trip that someone does alone
c. a voyage done only on water

B **Scan the article.** How long did Dave and Amy take to complete their journey?

C **Scan the article again.** Underline all the ways that Dave and Amy traveled.

ROUTE OF DAVE AND AMY'S JOURNEY

Kayak

Dogsled

Canoe

NORTH AMERICAN ODYSSEY.

🎧 1–18

Dave Freeman loves sports and exploration, and he wanted to teach students about the wonders of exploration and wilderness travel. However, it's impossible to take so many students on trips. So he had an idea—he would go on adventure trips to explore different places, 5 and share his experience with students through the Internet. The result of his idea was the Wilderness Classroom. Since then, Dave and his wife Amy have been exploring different parts of the world, and teaching students about the outdoors.

One of their most famous trips was called the North American 10 Odyssey. They wanted to use this journey to get people to protect North America's waterways and wild places. At the same time, they wanted to teach elementary and middle school students about these wild areas—their geography, history, wildlife, and so on.

The journey across North America began on April 22, 2010—Earth 15 Day. The Minnesotan couple began paddling their kayaks north out of Seattle. They spent the next three years kayaking, canoeing, dogsledding, and backpacking up the Inside Passage, across the Northwest Territories, through the Great Lakes, and down the East Coast of the United States.

20 Throughout the journey, about 85,000 students tracked Dave and Amy's progress. They made the Wilderness Classroom interactive and fun for these students. Every Monday during the trip, they posted an online update. They also posted videos every week. Students could help Dave and Amy make decisions about the trip by doing 25 surveys—they could suggest routes the couple should take. The couple was also able to interact with the kids at schools along the way. Over the three years of the project, they met around 25,000 students.

For Dave, who has been working as a guide for nearly 20 years, 30 "teaching kids when they're young that these places exist is a first stepping stone for getting people outside, understanding why these places are important, and working to protect them."

On April 4, 2013, Dave and Amy finally paddled into Key West, Florida, completing their North American Odyssey. But they haven't 35 been resting since then. They have been going on other adventures, continuing to teach students about exciting places outside the classroom.

Comprehension

IDIOM

If "the ball is in your court," it's time for you to _____.

a. share with a partner
b. let someone else finish
c. make a decision

A Answer the questions about *North American Odyssey*.

1. Detail   The Wilderness Classroom allows students to _____.

   a. plan a trip

   b. interact with wildlife

   c. learn about the outdoors

2. Main Idea   The second paragraph talks about the _____ of Dave and Amy's journey.

   a. difficulties

   b. goals

   c. outcome

3. Inference   The Wilderness Classroom idea makes the experience of wilderness travel more _____ students.

   a. pleasant for

   b. accessible to

   c. demanding for

4. Detail   Students helped Dave and Amy by _____.

   a. making suggestions

   b. giving money

   c. posting videos

5. Vocabulary   In line 31, a "stepping stone" is something that _____.

   a. is basic

   b. shows you the way

   c. helps you make progress

B Put the events in order (1–5).

_____ Dave and Amy decided to travel across North America.

_____ Dave and Amy began their three-year-long trip.

_____ Dave and Amy paddled into Key West, Florida.

_____ Dave and Amy posted updates and videos online.

_1_ The Wilderness Classroom was created.

C CRITICAL THINKING   **Talk with a partner.** Why do Dave and Amy want students to learn about and experience the wilderness? Would you like to learn through the Wilderness Classroom?

Writing

Write a biography.
Write about a famous athlete or adventurer.

| Home | BLOG | Photos | Contact | About Me |

Ryan Sheckler, Skateboarder
Ryan Sheckler is one of the world's youngest professional skateboarders. He has been skateboarding for most of his life. When he was six, his father encouraged him to learn skating. He has been practicing various tricks in his backyard since then. In 2008, he . . .

Life Rolls On

ABOUT THE VIDEO

Life Rolls On is an organization that has been inspiring people since 2002.

BEFORE YOU WATCH

Work with a partner. What do you think Life Rolls On does? Check (✓) the sentences you think describe the organization.

1. It makes wheelchairs for people with disabilities. ☐

2. It holds sports events for people with disabilities. ☐

3. It trains people with disabilities for sports competitions. ☐

4. It teaches people about spinal cord injury. ☐

WHILE YOU WATCH

A **Check your answers** to the Before You Watch question.

B **Watch the video again.** Match the people to their quotes.

1. ○ ○ a. "It's awesome that these people organize such events to push the limits, and I'm pretty stoked about it."

2. ○ ○ b. "I'm going to be surfing for the first time ever, and to be honest I never even thought that could be possible."

A participant at the "They Will Skate Again" event

3. ○ ○ c. "I get more back than I feel I could ever give."

AFTER YOU WATCH

Talk with a partner. Do you know organizations similar to Life Rolls On? What do they do?

YOU COULD ASK
FOR ADVICE.

A student speaking with a guidance counselor

Preview

A 🎧 1–19 **Listen.** Match the people to their problems.

1. Christine ○   ○ a. gets poor algebra grades
2. Kevin ○   ○ b. saw a classmate copying her answers
3. Daniel ○   ○ c. hates his friend's new look
4. Jenny ○   ○ d. has a broken laptop
5. Carlos ○   ○ e. lost his friend's comic book
6. Erica ○   ○ f. has a cousin who often borrows things
                               and doesn't return them

B 🎧 1–20 **Look at the phrases below.** Predict what advice the people will receive. Write the numbers (**1–6**). Three are extra. Then listen and check your answers.

_____ buy a new one   _____ say nothing   _____ get a tutor

_____ get it repaired   _____ tell the teacher   _____ go to the library

_____ apologize   _____ don't lend things   _____ talk to his friend

C **Talk with a partner.** Do you agree with the advice in **B**? If not, what advice would you give?

> I agree that Erica shouldn't lend things to her cousin anymore.

> Maybe she should have a talk with him.

Language Focus

A 🎧 1–21 **Listen and read.** Then repeat the conversation and replace the words in blue.

B **Practice with a partner.** Replace any words to make your own conversation.

🎧 1–22

GIVING ADVICE

My math grades aren't very good. What **should** I **do**?	You **should get** a private tutor. You **could join** a study group.
My friend won't talk to me because I told her I didn't like her new look.	You **could try apologizing** to her. **Have** you **tried apologizing**?
A classmate copied my answers.	**Why don't** you **tell** the teacher?
My friend always borrows my things without asking me first.	**If I were you**, I'd tell him that you're uncomfortable about it.

C Circle the correct answers.

1. My brother always plays his music loudly, and I can't study. What (**could** / **should**) I do?

2. They want to make our school more beautiful. Maybe they (**could** / **would**) paint a wall mural.

3. It's hard for Talia to make friends. She doesn't know what she (**would** / **should**) do.

4. I heard you want to do volunteer work with animals. If I were you, I (**could** / **would**) contact the local animal shelter.

5. Our school doesn't recycle much. What (**could** / **would**) we do to encourage recycling?

D 🎧1–23 **Complete the conversation.** Then listen and check your answers.

David: Are you OK, Gina?

Gina: Oh, yeah. It's my brother. He's been playing video games a lot lately. He doesn't talk to anyone and even skips meals sometimes.

David: 1. (**to stop** / **have** / **tried asking** / **him** / **you**) _____ ?

Gina: I have. But he didn't really listen to me.

David: 2. (**talk** / **his** / **don't** / **you** / **friends** / **to** / **why**) _____ ?

Gina: 3. (**say** / **I** / **what** / **should**) _____ ?

David: 4. (**could** / **if** / **you** / **been** / **ask** / **them** / **feeling** / **he's** / **stressed** / **recently**)

_____ .

Gina: OK. Maybe 5. (**him** / **could** / **they** / **as well** / **to** / **talk**) _____ .

E **Give advice.** Write an example for each category. Then turn to page 126 and follow the instructions.

1. a family member   _____

2. something you wear (plural)   _____

3. another thing you wear (plural)   _____

4. a color   _____

5. a healthy food (plural)   _____

6. an unhealthy food (non-count)   _____

7. a sport   _____

The Real World

Picturing the
World

Annie Griffiths is an award-winning National Geographic photographer. Throughout her career, she has traveled to over a hundred countries. She often takes photos for charity organizations around the world.

A 🎧1–24 **Listen.** Circle **T** for True or **F** for False.

1. Griffiths always wanted to be a photographer.   **T**   **F**

2. Griffiths started working for National Geographic while she was in college.   **T**   **F**

3. Griffiths' first photo for National Geographic was of hail damage.   **T**   **F**

4. Griffiths found transportation to be a challenging part of her job   **T**   **F**
   at National Geographic.

B 🎧1–24 **Listen again.** Complete the advice Griffiths gives.

1. "I think young people should _____ very different from where they live."

2. "If I were a teenager again, I'd spend more time developing

   _____."

3. "Someone who is looking for their dream job should spend time with

   _____."

Discussion. Work in a group. Tell your group about your dream job. Then ask them for advice on how to achieve your dream.

Pronunciation

Weak form of *should* and *could*

A 🎧1-25 **Listen and repeat.**

1. You could go to art school.

2. You should try talking to him.

B 🎧1-26 **Listen.** Complete the sentences.

1. You _____ to your teacher about it.

2. You _____ your parents for advice.

3. I think you _____ your friend now and apologize.

4. You _____ to raise money by having a charity fair.

5. You _____ to art school if you want to be a photographer.

6. Everyone here _____ more to protect the environment.

C **Work with a partner.** Take turns to read the sentences in **B**.

DO YOU KNOW?

Which famous person failed his university entrance exam?

a. Albert Einstein
b. Steve Jobs
c. Barack Obama

Communication

Ask for and give advice. Work with a partner. Choose a problem below. Take turns asking for and giving advice.

A friend recently stopped talking to me, and I don't know why.

I saw the answers to tomorrow's science test.

My friend copies everything I do.

I want to get a part-time job, but my parents don't want me to.

I want to be a movie star when I finish school.

I don't like my new haircut.

My best friend is moving away to another city.

I would like to be more talkative and outgoing around people.

I want to get a part-time job, but my parents don't want me to. What should I do?

You could tell them about the things you can learn by having a part-time job.

Molly Burke speaking at
We Day in Toronto, Canada

Reading

A **Scan the article.** When did
Molly lose her sight?

B **Skim the article.** What made
Molly join Me to We?

C **Talk with a partner.** How do
you think Molly overcame her
problem of being bullied?

VISION OF
HOPE 🎧1-27

Molly Burke was not born blind. She started losing her sight when she was four years old. Doctors said that she had a rare eye disease that would slowly take away her vision completely. In first grade, she learned to read Braille, although she could still see. Life was pretty
5 normal for the next few years. However, in seventh grade, things got worse. Black turned to gray. Yellow turned to white. Soon, Molly couldn't see the blackboard.

"I just started to cry," remembers Molly. Her parents told her everything would be OK. "But I knew it wouldn't." As her vision faded, Molly started
10 using a cane to help her walk. This embarrassed her friends, and people stopped inviting her to do things. Then the bullying began.

Molly once broke her ankle and had to use crutches to help her walk. A group of girls—girls who were once her friends—committed a terrible act of bullying. They were usually responsible for walking
15 Molly to the cafeteria. Instead, they took the blind 14-year-old outside and down a hill. They smashed Molly's crutches against a tree and ran away. "I was alone," remembers Molly. "I couldn't see. I couldn't walk." Luckily, Molly had her cell phone and was able to call her mother for help.

20 After she finished high school, Molly thought about what she wanted to do before going to college. Her brother was working in a children's home in Africa, and she wanted to do something that would help others, too. Then, she found out about Me to We, an organization that has been helping people through volunteering
25 and developing leadership skills. She joined the organization on a youth trip to Kenya to help build a school. While there, she spoke at a local girls' school. Molly now knew what she wanted to do next—to be one of the motivational speakers at Me to We.

Molly has been speaking to schools all over the United States and
30 Canada about bullying. Her advice? Be strong! During a speech in Toronto, she spoke to about 20,000 people. They stood up and clapped wildly after her speech. Her father said, "Molly has a real ability to inspire people and to help others who are going through something, whether it's a disability, or bullying, or a different set of challenges."

35 "Four years ago, no one even wanted to sit near me, and people thought I wasn't worth anything," said Molly. "Now there are 20,000 people on their feet supporting me. It's a really cool feeling."

Comprehension

A Answer the questions about *Vision of Hope*.

1. **Detail** Molly learned Braille because she _____.

    a. was blind

    b. was interested in it

    c. would be blind someday

2. **Reference** In line 10, "this" refers to Molly's _____.

    a. walking

    b. use of a cane

    c. fading vision

3. **Inference** People bullied Molly because they didn't like _____.

    a. her personality

    b. helping her

    c. that she was different

4. **Vocabulary** In line 16, "smashed" means _____.

    a. broke

    b. placed

    c. hid

5. **Inference** Molly is sharing her own experience to help other people _____.

    a. be leaders

    b. challenge themselves

    c. overcome their problems

IDIOM

To "pull the wool over someone's eyes" means to _____ someone.

a. bully

b. blind

c. trick

B **Complete the timeline.** Write the letters of the events below.

> a. experienced bullying
> b. started losing her sight
> c. went on a youth trip to Kenya
> d. learned to read Braille
> e. completely lost her vision
> f. speaks for Me to We

In seventh grade   After high school graduation

Age 4   In first grade   Age 14   Now

C **CRITICAL THINKING** **Talk with a partner.** Do you know someone who was bullied? What do you think people should do if they are being bullied?

Writing

Write a letter to yourself from four years ago. Give yourself advice.

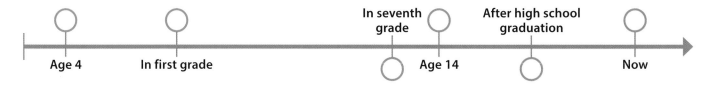

Home	BLOG	Photos	Contact	About Me

Dear Walt,

I'm writing this letter to you, my 14-year-old self. I'm currently 18 years old, and I think I can offer you some good advice. High school is a difficult time. But you shouldn't be afraid to fail. You should also study hard. If I were 14 again, I'd try to get good grades in every class. Finally, you shouldn't listen to bullies . . .

Eco-Fuel Africa

ABOUT THE VIDEO

National Geographic Explorer Sanga Moses wants to improve the lives of people in Uganda.

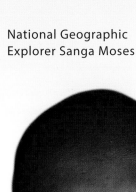

National Geographic Explorer Sanga Moses

BEFORE YOU WATCH

What do you know about Uganda? Circle the correct answers.

1. The capital city of Uganda is (**Kira** / **Kampala**).

2. Uganda's biggest export is (**coffee** / **fuel**).

3. About (**40** / **80**) percent of the population live in rural areas.

4. (**English** / **French**) is one of the national languages of Uganda.

WHILE YOU WATCH

A **Circle the correct answers.**

1. Many children in Uganda don't have time for school because they need to (**cook** / **gather wood**) for their families.

2. The eco-fuel is made from (**cheaper wood** / **farm waste**).

3. Eco-Fuel Africa helps farmers and women (**earn more income** / **get an education**).

B **Watch the video again.** What are the advantages of Moses' eco-fuel? Check (✓) the ones mentioned in the video.

◯ burns cleaner   ◯ saves forests   ◯ creates a bigger fire

◯ burns longer   ◯ cheaper   ◯ can be reused many times

AFTER YOU WATCH

Talk with a partner. Are there any environmental issues in your country? What could you do about them?

4

THE KOALA WAS TAKEN TO A SHELTER.

Preview

A 🎧 1–28 **Listen.** Check (✓) the things that are done when an animal is found.

- ☐ It's wrapped in a blanket.
- ☐ It's given food.
- ☐ It's placed in a cage.
- ☐ It's driven to the shelter.
- ☐ It's washed.
- ☐ A tag is attached to it.

B 🎧 1–28 **Listen again.** Circle the correct answers.

1. Wrapping the koala in a blanket helps (**make it sleep** / **calm it down**).

2. It's easier to (**check for injuries on** / **feed**) the koala after washing it.

3. Tags are attached to koalas to (**monitor their health** / **identify them**).

C **Talk with a partner.** Have you ever seen, or read a story about, an injured or lost animal? Explain what happened.

> I found a kitten behind my house once. It was abandoned.

> How sad. What did you do?

A koala's cast being trimmed by a vet from the Australia Zoo Wildlife Hospital

Language Focus

A 🎧1-29 **Listen and read.** Then repeat the conversation and replace the words in **blue**.

REAL ENGLISH It's up to you.

B **Practice with a partner.** Replace any words to make your own conversation.

🎧1-30

TALKING ABOUT THINGS THAT WERE DONE	
A volunteer **wraps** the bird in a blanket.	The bird **is wrapped** in a blanket.
He **brought** an injured animal into the shelter yesterday.	An injured animal **was brought** into the shelter yesterday.
The vet **checked** the cats for any injuries.	The cats **were checked** for any injuries.
The rescue center **has released** the sloth back into the wild.	The sloth **has been released** back into the wild.
Is an injured animal **given** medicine?	Yes, it **is**. / No, it **isn't**.
Were the dogs **brought** in yesterday?	Yes, they **were**. / No, they **weren't**.

C **Complete the conversation.** Use the correct forms of the words in parentheses.

Max: How was your weekend, Chloe?

Chloe: Very interesting. I volunteered at the animal shelter.

Max: Really? Was it a good experience?

Chloe: It was! On Saturday, a baby bird (1) _____ (**bring**) in. Everyone thought it had a broken wing.

Max: (2) _____ it _____ (**abandon**)? I heard mother birds do that sometimes.

Chloe: Yeah. It (3) _____ (**give**) some medicine, and then the vet checked its wing. The vet said its wing wasn't broken.

Max: Well, that's good. (4) _____ it _____ (**release**) then?

Chloe: No, it's still a little young. I think they're planning to keep it for a while. I also helped with two raccoons. They (5) _____ (**hit**) by a car.

Max: Oh, no. Did they survive?

Chloe: Yeah, they (6) _____ (**treat**) for leg and chest injuries. They will have to stay there until they get better.

D 🎧1–31 **Complete the sentences.** Use the correct forms of the words in parentheses. Then listen and check your answers.

If you find a small injured animal like a bird or squirrel, it probably (1) _____ (**abandon**). Before you (2) _____ (**take**) the animal to a shelter, gently cover it with a towel or blanket. Then try to get it into a box or cage.

Line a box with paper, a towel, or a shirt to make the animal more comfortable. Move it to a dark, quiet place. Once it (3) _____ (**put**) in a dark place, it will begin to relax. Don't feed the animal.

You should (4) _____ (**call**) for help if you find a larger animal like a deer or raccoon. Never approach larger wild animals unless you (5) _____ (**tell**) to do so.

E **Complete a story about a rescued animal.** Work with a partner. **Student A:** Turn to page 126. **Student B:** Turn to page 128.

A volunteer checking on a rescued bird

The Photo Ark

The Photo Ark project is an online archive of photos of endangered zoo animals. Created by National Geographic photographer Joel Sartore in 2005, it has photos of several thousand animals.

A 🎧1–32 **Listen.** Check (✓) the topics that are discussed.

- ◯ types of animals in the Photo Ark
- ◯ the goal of the Photo Ark project
- ◯ where Sartore photographs animals
- ◯ the challenge of photographing animals
- ◯ Sartore's favorite animal to photograph
- ◯ ways to support Sartore's work

B 🎧1–32 **Listen again.** Circle the correct answers.

1. The Photo Ark project aims to (**raise awareness of animal extinction** / **record all the plants and animals in the world**).

2. Some of the animals in the Photo Ark have (**become extinct** / **been adopted**).

3. Animals in the Photo Ark are photographed (**in their natural environment** / **against a plain background**).

4. Sartore (**believes** / **doesn't believe**) that some endangered animals are more important than others.

5. One way to support Sartore's work is to (**visit zoos** / **adopt a rescued animal**).

CRITICAL THINKING Some people think that animals shouldn't be kept in zoos or aquariums. Instead, they should be free. What do you think? Are zoos protecting animals, or harming them?

Pronunciation
Intonation in a series

A 🎧 1-33 **Listen and repeat.**

1. The shelter was able to save a bird, a raccoon, and a rabbit.

2. The koala was wrapped in a blanket, given water, and washed.

B 🎧 1-34 **Work with a partner.** Take turns reading the sentences below. Then listen and check your intonation.

1. The baby bear was trapped, scared, and hungry.

2. The bird was picked up, wrapped in a blanket, and taken to the shelter.

3. The animal was given food, water, and medicine.

4. The shelter accepts donations of food, blankets, and money.

5. The injured fox was carefully picked up, placed in a cage, and put in a dark place.

C **Complete the sentences.** Then read them to a partner.

1. After I get home from class, I _____, _____, and _____.

2. The three people I'm closest to are _____, _____, and _____.

3. This weekend, I plan to _____, _____, and _____.

Communication

Present a news story. Work in a group. Choose one of the headlines below or make up your own. Include detailed information to make the story interesting. Present your group's news story to the class.

Monkey Spotted at Playground

Thirty Cats Rescued from Burning Building

Rabbit Found Wearing Clothes

Teenagers Hurt at Zoo

Deer Discovered in High School Cafeteria

TOWN'S PET FISH RELEASED INTO RIVER

A large deer was discovered last night in a high school cafeteria.

That's right. A guard heard a noise in the cafeteria and went to see. The deer was seen eating potato chips.

Reading

A **Look at the photos.** What do you think happened?

B **Scan the article.** Where did the bear spend the night?

C **Skim the article.** Underline all the people who were involved in the rescue.

A black bear hanging onto the arch of a bridge in California

Rescuers use a net to carry the bear.

BEAR
RESCUE 🎧 1–35

A black bear was in a dangerous situation when she fell off a 30-meter-high bridge. After a long day in California's Sierra Nevada mountains, the bear probably thought she was taking a shortcut home. She was walking across the bridge when, suddenly, two cars
5 entered from both sides. There was nowhere to run, so the frightened bear jumped onto the rail and began to fall over the side.

Luckily, the bear pulled herself onto an arch under the bridge, but she was trapped there. A driver saw the unbelievable scene and called 911. Robert Brooks, an animal control officer from the nearby
10 town of Truckee, was sent to investigate. "I thought it was a joke," he said. But it wasn't a joke, so he called Dave Baker of the BEAR League—a group that helps bears in trouble. "He thought I was playing a joke on him, too," Brooks said.

Unfortunately, the sky was getting dark, so the rescuers had to wait.
15 Early next morning, the two men returned to the bridge with more volunteers. Amazingly, the bear was still there. They needed to rescue her quickly. Baker had an idea—they should hang a net under the bear, push her into it, and then lower her to the ground.

Firefighters volunteered to lower the 100-kilogram bear once she
20 was in the net. Police officers closed the road, and when the net arrived, it was hung under the bridge. Then, an animal control officer shot a dart containing a sleeping drug into the bear's shoulder. Ann Bryant, head of the BEAR League, stood under the bridge. When the bear was sleepy, Bryant yelled, "OK, push!" A volunteer rock climber
25 used his feet to push the bear off the arch, right into the middle of the net.

The bear was gently lowered to the ground. When she touched the ground, everyone cheered. Bryant and Officer Brooks guided the sleepy bear to a stream, where she could finally get a drink. "She just
30 kind of lay down on her tummy and put her paws under her chin," said Bryant, "like a dog lying on the living room floor . . . only big!" The rescuers then cleared all the people from the area and left the bear alone so she could sleep. Since then, no one has seen her. "I don't think she's going near that bridge anymore," Brooks said.

Comprehension

A Answer the questions about *Bear Rescue*.

1. Purpose   The purpose of the article is to _____ .

   a. teach readers about bears

   b. tell an interesting story

   c. persuade readers that wild bears are dangerous

2. Detail   The bear climbed onto the rail because she was _____ .

   a. scared   b. lost   c. curious

3. Inference   Baker thought Brooks was joking because _____ .

   a. it was an unbelievable story

   b. Brooks often tells jokes

   c. it was a very funny story

IDIOM

To "be out of harm's way" means to be _____ .

a. healthy
b. safe
c. far away

4. Inference   The rescuers had to make the bear sleep first so that she _____ .

   a. could rest

   b. wouldn't be hungry

   c. wouldn't attack people

5. Vocabulary   A "stream" is a _____ . (line 29)

   a. pool   b. small river   c. lake

B Circle six sentences that best summarize the article. Then put them in order (**1–6**). Two sentences are extra.

a. _____ The bear was lowered safely to the ground.

b. _____ Rescuers hung a net under the bridge.

c. _____ The scared bear weighed 100 kilograms.

d. _____ The bear started to fall and became stuck under the bridge.

e. _____ The people who were watching were all cleared from the area.

f. _1_ A bear was walking across a tall bridge in the Sierra Nevada mountains.

g. _____ The bear was shot with a sleeping dart and pushed into the net.

h. _____ Two cars entered the bridge, and the bear jumped onto the rail.

C Talk with a partner. Are there wild bears in your country? Do you know what you should do if you encounter a wild bear?

Writing

Write a news article. Look at this photo and describe what you think happened.

Animal Portraits

ABOUT THE VIDEO

Joel Sartore has been photographing animals for the Photo Ark project since 2005.

BEFORE YOU WATCH

Talk with a partner. What do you remember about the Photo Ark?

1. What is the aim of Joel Sartore's Photo Ark project?

2. Where are the photographs of the animals taken?

3. How many species has Sartore photographed so far?

WHILE YOU WATCH

A **Check your answers to the Before You Watch questions.**

B **Watch the video again.** Circle the correct answers.

1. Sartore's projects mainly deal with _____.

   a. conservation   b. illegal killing of animals

2. The animals are photographed against black or white backgrounds because it _____.

   a. calms the animals down   b. allows us to focus on them

3. Sartore feels that his project _____.

   a. is near completion   b. will continue for a long time

AFTER YOU WATCH

Talk with a partner. What endangered animals do you know? What other things can we do to stop them from becoming extinct?

Joel Sartore with a clouded leopard

HOW WAS IT
FORMED?

Wave Rock, Australia

Queen's Head Rock, Taiwan

Preview

A 🎧2-01 **Listen.** How were the rock formations below created? Check (✓) the correct answers.

	eaten away by water	worn down by wind	formed by volcanoes	broken apart by ice
1. Wave Rock	◯	◯	◯	◯
2. Queen's Head Rock	◯	◯	◯	◯
3. Rock Towers	◯	◯	◯	◯

B 🎧2-01 **Listen again.** Circle **T** for True or **F** for False.

1. The colored stripes on Wave Rock were created by rain.   **T**   **F**

2. Queen's Head Rock is in danger of falling over.   **T**   **F**

3. The Turkish rock towers are now closed to visitors.   **T**   **F**

C **Talk with a partner.** Do you know any interesting rock formations?

> The rock pillars on Jeju island in South Korea have an interesting shape.

> Do you know how they were formed?

Language Focus

A 🎧 2-02 **Listen and read.** Then repeat the conversation and replace the words in blue.

B **Practice with a partner.** Replace any words to make your own conversation.

1 Wow! Look at that rock, Ming!

That's the famous Elephant Trunk Hill. Can you see its **trunk**?

eyes
leg

2 No. Oh, wait! There it is.

It's been **eaten away** by wind and water for millions of years.

worn down
shaped

3 It was probably worn down by the wind, too.

Look at that **amazing** rock! It looks like a camel.

incredible
interesting

4 Guilin is a great place to study **geology**!

Yeah. Maybe in a million years that camel will look like a tiny squirrel!

rocks
nature

🎧 2-03

TALKING ABOUT HOW THINGS WERE DONE

Glaciers **form** valleys.	Valleys **are formed by** glaciers.
The sea **is washing away** the beach.	The beach **is being washed away by** the sea.
Ice **broke apart** the rock.	The rock **was broken apart by** ice.
Water **has eaten away** the canyon.	The canyon **has been eaten away by** water.
How **were** these cracks **made**?	They **were made by** an earthquake.
Was Elephant Trunk Hill **created by humans**?	No. It **was shaped by** wind and water.

C 🎧2–04 **Complete the sentences.** Use the correct forms of the words in the box. Then listen and check your answers.

| agree on | ~~eat away~~ | put out | look after | pull over | tear down |

1. Look at these canyon walls. They __have been eaten away__ by wind and water for many years.

2. The red car _____ by the police because it was going too fast.

3. To protect the plants and animals in the area, a plan to create a national park _____ by the government.

4. The children _____ by their grandmother when their parents are at work.

5. After last year's hurricane, many damaged homes _____ by the government.

6. Finally, after ten hours, the fire _____ by the firefighters.

D **Complete the sentences.** Use the correct forms of the words in parentheses.

Utah's Landscape Arch (1) _____ (**consider**) by many people to be one of the most beautiful natural arches in the world. It (2) _____ (**name**) by Frank Beckwith, an expedition leader who (3) _____ (**explore**) the area in the winter of 1933–34. The arch is 88 meters long. In 1991, a large piece of rock (4) _____ (**fall**) from the thinnest part of the arch. This (5) _____ (**capture**) on video by a tourist. In 1995, another piece fell. Unfortunately, this (6) _____ (**cause**) the arch to become unstable, so the path under it (7) _____ (**close**) by the park service. The thinnest part of the arch is now less than two meters thick.

E **Work with a partner. Student A:** Turn to page 127. **Student B:** Turn to page 130.

Landscape Arch in Utah, U.S.A.

The Real World

Supervolcano

Volcanoes are powerful. The force of a volcanic eruption can cover a great area of land with rocks and lava. But there's something that could be more dangerous when it erupts— a supervolcano.

Eyjafjallajökull volcano in Iceland

A 🎧2–05 **Listen.** Complete the sentences.

1. A volcanic eruption happens when hot lava and gas escape to the Earth's _____.

2. Big volcanic eruptions can affect the _____.

3. The average temperature worldwide _____ after Mount Pinatubo erupted.

4. The eruption of the Icelandic volcano caused the biggest air travel disruption since _____.

B 🎧2–06 **Listen.** Circle **T** for True or **F** for False.

1. A supervolcano can be easily seen because it's huge.　　**T F**

2. Hot, molten rock is trapped underground in a supervolcano.　　**T F**

3. Plant and animal species can become extinct if a supervolcano erupts.　　**T F**

4. Yellowstone's supervolcano erupted recently.　　**T F**

CRITICAL THINKING　Many people choose to live near active volcanoes although it is dangerous. Why do you think they choose to take such a risk?

Pronunciation
Contrastive stress

A 🎧2-07 **Listen and repeat.**

1. Did the rock chamber explode?   No, it **collapsed**.
2. I think this rock was shaped by wind.   Actually, it was by **water**.
3. Is Pluto a planet?   It **was** considered a planet, but not anymore.

B 🎧2-08 **Underline the stressed words in the responses.** Then listen and check your answers.

1. Are the rock towers in Taiwan?   No, they're in Turkey.
2. I think heat broke this rock apart.   Actually, ice broke it apart.
3. Are the glaciers continuing to grow?   No, they're actually melting very quickly.

C **Work with a partner.** Take turns to read the sentences in **B**.

DO YOU KNOW?

Pumice, a type of volcanic rock, is sometimes used ____ .

a. as fuel in barbecues
b. to make paper
c. in beauty products

Communication

Find the people below. When you find the person, ask a follow-up question to get additional information.

Find someone who . . .	Additional Information
was named after a relative.	_____
has seen a volcano.	_____
has been chased by a dog.	_____
has visited a natural wonder.	_____
has been awarded a prize.	_____
has been stung by a bee.	_____
has been tricked by someone.	_____

Were you named after a relative?

Who were you named after?

Yes, I was.

I was named after my uncle.

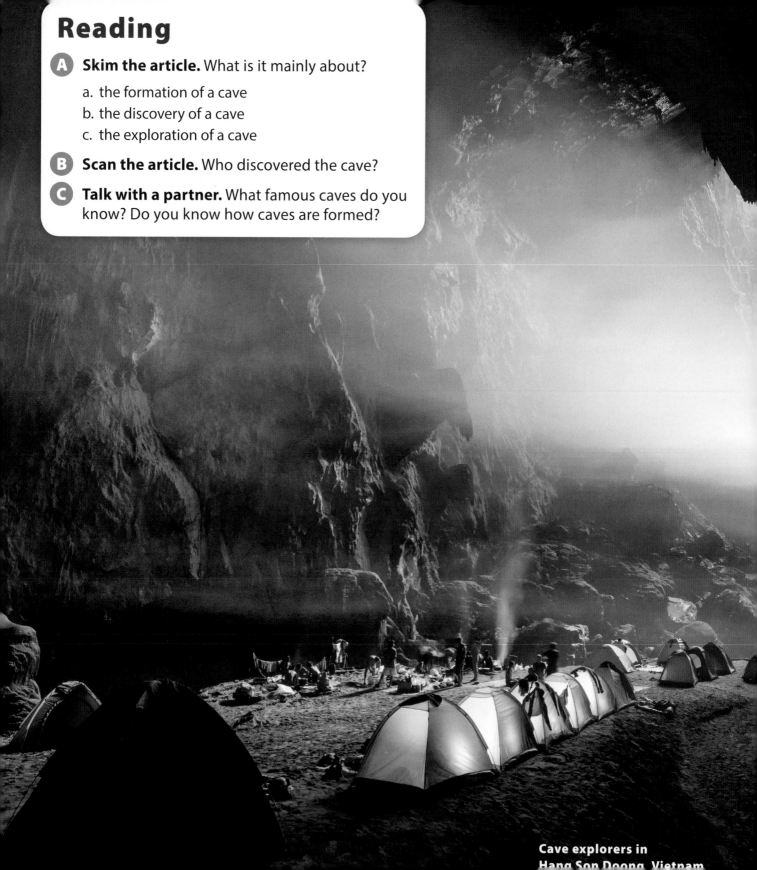

Reading

A **Skim the article.** What is it mainly about?

   a. the formation of a cave
   b. the discovery of a cave
   c. the exploration of a cave

B **Scan the article.** Who discovered the cave?

C **Talk with a partner.** What famous caves do you know? Do you know how caves are formed?

Cave explorers in
Hang Son Doong, Vietnam

CAVE OF SECRETS

🎧 2–09

A team of scientists and cave experts stand at the entrance of Hang Son Doong—the world's largest cave. Hidden deep in the dense mountain jungle of central Vietnam, the cave was created millions of years ago when rock under the mountain was eroded by river water.
5 The weakened rock eventually collapsed, creating a massive underworld now waiting to be explored.

Hang Son Doong, which means "mountain river cave," was discovered by a local man named Ho Khanh in 1991, but it wasn't until 2009 that a group of British cavers explored it for the first time. The cavers had to
10 stop after four kilometers because a great wall blocked their way. But now, a year later, they have returned to climb past the wall and find out where the cave ends.

Inside, the team determines that in some sections, the cave soars more than 180 meters high and spreads almost 90 meters wide. An
15 entire New York City block—complete with 40-story skyscrapers—could fit inside the cave. There are even misty clouds above—the cave is so large that it has its own weather system!

Deeper in the cave, the team members fight to keep their balance as they walk slowly through an underground river. Then they make
20 their way through a field of huge rocks—some the size of houses. The team reaches an area where the cave's roof has fallen in, creating two spectacular natural skylights. An explorer says, "Watch out for dinosaurs" as his partner walks into the light. In this dreamy place, prehistoric reptiles seem likely to appear at any moment.

25 The team scrambles around wet, slippery rock formations as they try to make their way toward the second skylight. They walk carefully here because a wrong step can lead to a fall of over 30 meters. The second, larger hole in the ceiling has brought down some of the jungle with it. A fantastic forest of trees rises toward the bright sun
30 above. Monkeys, snakes, and birds live in this part of the cave jungle.

Further inside, the team slogs through a thick, muddy trench. The team's final hurdle is its toughest challenge—they climb up a slimy 60-meter cliff made of hard minerals. After a two-day climb, they literally see light at the end of the tunnel as they reach the cave's
35 exit. Satisfied with the expedition to explore, map, and photograph the world's largest cave, the team climbs out into the sunlight. They have become the first people to explore the entire length of the cave.

Comprehension

A **Answer the questions about *Cave of Secrets*.**

1. `Inference` The cave wasn't known until recently because the entrance was _____.

   a. hidden

   b. blocked by a wall

   c. deep underground

2. `Detail` Clouds are formed in the cave due to its _____.

   a. depth   b. location   c. size

3. `Inference` Why does the explorer say, "Watch out for dinosaurs"?

   a. Dinosaurs used to live in the cave.

   b. The cave feels like a different world.

   c. The explorers were looking for dinosaur bones.

4. `Vocabulary` To "see light at the end of the tunnel" means to _____ something. (line 34)

   a. imagine

   b. understand

   c. be close to completing

5. `Detail` Cavers successfully explored the whole cave in _____.

   a. 2009   b. 2010   c. 2011

IDIOM

To "cave in" means to _____ something.

a. reluctantly agree to
b. be angry about
c. find out about

B **CRITICAL THINKING** **Find the words below in the article.** Group them in the chart according to their meanings.

| soars | scramble | slippery | slogs | muddy |
| spectacular | dreamy | fantastic | hurdle | slimy |

More Positive	More Negative

C **Talk with a partner.** Do you think Hang Son Doong should be open to the public for tours? Why or why not?

Writing

Create a tourist guide. Describe an interesting landscape and give information about how it was formed.

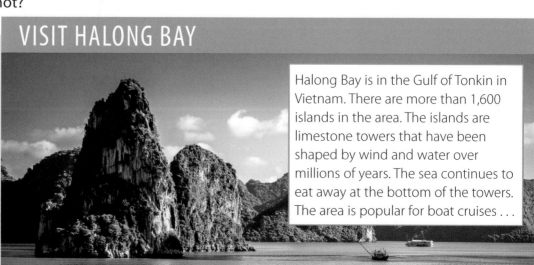

VISIT HALONG BAY

Halong Bay is in the Gulf of Tonkin in Vietnam. There are more than 1,600 islands in the area. The islands are limestone towers that have been shaped by wind and water over millions of years. The sea continues to eat away at the bottom of the towers. The area is popular for boat cruises . . .

Mountain River Cave

ABOUT THE VIDEO

Ryan Deboodt took an amazing video of Hang Son Doong when he visited in 2014.

Cave explorers at Hang Son Doong

BEFORE YOU WATCH

What do you remember about Hang Son Doong? Circle the correct answers.

1. It was formed by a (**river** / **volcano**).

2. It's in (**Cambodia** / **Vietnam**).

3. It was first explored by (**British** / **American**) cavers.

WHILE YOU WATCH

A Check your answers to the Before You Watch questions.

B Watch the video again. Circle **T** for True or **F** for False.

1. Deboodt stayed in the cave for eight days to make the video.	T	F
2. Deboodt made the video by climbing up the cave walls.	T	F
3. Fossils that are 300 million years old have been found in the cave.	T	F
4. The cave is not yet open to the public.	T	F

AFTER YOU WATCH

Talk with a partner. Would you like to visit Hang Son Doong? What are the most amazing places you've visited?

LOOK AT THAT
NARWHAL!

A narwhal, which is a type of whale, is sometimes known as the "unicorn of the sea."

Preview

A 🎧 2-10 **Listen.** Write the ocean(s) each animal lives in: Atlantic (**At**),
Pacific (**P**), Indian (**I**), Arctic (**Ar**), or Southern (**S**).

1. dugong _____   2. king crab _____   3. narwhal _____

4. penguin _____   5. seahorse _____

B 🎧 2-10 **Listen again.** Complete the sentences.

> feathers   flippers   shells   tail   tusk

1. The dugong uses its _____ to swim.

2. King crabs, which can have blue, red, or gold _____, are caught
   for food.

3. The narwhal, which has a long, straight _____, is a type of whale.

4. Penguins, which have short, dense _____, are highly adapted for
   life in the Antarctic.

5. The seahorse, which is a type of fish, uses its _____ to move
   forward.

C **Talk with a partner.** Describe an interesting sea creature you know.

> The octopus can lose one of its arms when
> escaping from danger. It regrows its arm later.

> Male seahorses give birth
> and care for their young.

Language Focus

A 🎧 **2-11** **Listen and read.** Then repeat the conversation and replace the words in blue.

B **Practice with a partner.** Replace any words to make your own conversation.

1 Look! That shell is moving!

Oh, that's a hermit crab. **They're really common** here.

You see them everywhere
You find them all over the beach

2 I've never seen one before.

Its shell, **which is for protection**, is an abandoned seashell.

which is its home
which it lives in

3 Really? Do they live in the same shell all their lives?

No, they change shells. It's **incredible** to watch.

amazing
interesting

4 If they don't like their new shell, they go back to the old one.

So, you're telling me they want the most **fashionable** shell-ter!

stylish
up-to-date

🎧 **2-12**

ADDING INFORMATION ABOUT THINGS AND PEOPLE

The narwhal, **which is a type of whale**, has a long, straight tusk.

The dugong, **which is a kind of mammal**, is sometimes called a sea cow.

Last weekend we went to the aquarium, **which now has a collection of seahorses**.

My uncle, **who visits every summer**, is a marine biologist.

My cousin Lisa, **who is a scuba diving instructor**, knows a lot about coral reefs.

If you have questions, ask the tour guide, **who is an expert on ocean conservation**.

C 🎧 2-13 **Complete the sentences.** Write the letters of the phrases in the box. Then listen and check your answers.

> a. who sell jellyfish to restaurants in the region   b. which is faster than a person walks
>
> c. which are inside their bell-shaped bodies   d. which live in oceans around the world

Jellyfish are interesting sea creatures. They have been around for millions of years, even before dinosaurs lived on Earth. These creatures, (1) _____, have a life span of about a year. They eat fish, shrimp, crabs, and tiny plants. Jellyfish use their mouths, (2) _____, to eat and move—they squirt water from their mouths to move forward. The jellyfish is a very efficient swimmer, and swims at a speed of about 8 km/h, (3) _____. Jellyfish are sometimes caught by people for food. Fishermen in Southeast Asia, (4) _____, are usually busy during the jellyfish seasons—between March and May and August and November.

D **Rewrite the sentences.** Use *which* or *who*.

1. Whale sharks are the world's largest fish. They are shy and gentle.

   <u>Whale sharks, which are shy and gentle, are the world's largest fish.</u>

2. Coral reefs are an important habitat for millions of animals. They are like underwater cities.

   _____

3. My uncle showed us some manta rays. He works at the aquarium.

   _____

4. *Titanic* is now an underwater shelter for marine life. It sank in 1912.

   _____

5. Alice wants to write a research paper on dugongs. She's a marine biologist.

   _____

E **Play a chain game.** Work in a group of three. At each turn, add more information to the sentence using *which* or *who*.

> Jun is from Seoul.

> Jun, who is our classmate, is from Seoul.

Marine Inspirations

Sometimes, we can get inspiration from nature. People study birds, for example, to learn more about flight. By studying plants and animals—how they live or move—we might be able to find creative ways to build things.

A 🎧 2-14 **Listen.** Complete the sentences.

1. Mercedes-Benz modeled their Bionic Car on the shape of a kind of _____.

2. The large front area of the car allows it to drive more smoothly in the _____.

3. The Seabreacher is a kind of _____ vehicle that copies the way marine animals swim.

A Mercedes-Benz Bionic Car

B 🎧 2-14 **Listen again.** Classify the features below. Write **B** for the Bionic Car or **S** for the Seabreacher. There may be more than one answer.

1. _____ Fits more than two people

2. _____ Is able to dive into the water

3. _____ Has a similar shape to marine animals

4. _____ Can travel up to almost 200 km/h

CRITICAL THINKING Which animals and plants do you think we can study so that we can copy their features?

Pronunciation
Relative clauses

A 🎧 2-15 **Listen and repeat.**

1. Maria, who is the director of this aquarium, is very interested in marine conservation.

2. Ostriches, which can live for more than 40 years, are the largest birds on Earth.

B 🎧 2-16 **Look at the sentences below.** Add commas where necessary. Then listen and check your answers.

1. Saltwater crocodiles which are very dangerous are the largest living reptiles.

2. Cynthia who is one of my best friends visits us every summer.

3. These seal pups which are three weeks old were washed away by a storm.

4. Tom who has been studying coral reefs is giving a presentation on them next week.

5. Sea otters which live in the Pacific Ocean are very playful animals.

C **Work with a partner.** Take turns to read the sentences in **B**.

DO YOU KNOW?

Some species of _____ mate for life.
a. sea otter
b. albatross
c. hermit crab

Communication

Play a guessing game. Work in a group. **Group A:** Turn to page 129. **Group B:** Turn to page 131. Follow the instructions on the page.

This animal, which has a life span of about 23 years, lives in the Pacific Ocean.

Is it a whale shark?

No, sorry. Here's another clue. It eats for three hours a day to stay warm.

Reading

A **Look at the title and the photos.** What do you think the article is about?

B **Skim the article.** Write the letters of the subheadings in the correct places.

    a. Reefs in Trouble   b. Big Challenges

    c. Supersize Cities   d. Why Are Reefs Important?

C **Talk with a partner.** Do you think coral reefs are important to us? Why?

Coral polyps

The Great Barrier
Reef in Australia

CITIES
in the SEA 🎧 2-17

They may be small, but they build big things! Coral polyps, which live in the warm, shallow parts of the Earth's oceans, are probably the biggest builders on the planet. Coral polyps turn calcium from seawater into a hard material called limestone.
Slowly, they build up a hard skeleton around their bodies. When polyps die, their
5 skeletons remain. Young polyps attach themselves to the old skeletons and make new skeletons. Over time, weird and wonderful shapes are slowly built up into amazing coral reefs.

_____ Some coral reefs are huge, and the Great Barrier Reef in Australia is the largest of them all. It covers 350,000 square kilometers.

10 Scientists sometimes think of coral reefs as underwater cities. A quarter of all known marine species live in reef habitats—there are nearly a thousand coral species. Reefs are also home to millions of sea creatures, like fish, crabs, turtles, and sharks.

_____ Humans don't live in coral reef cities, but we benefit from them. Reefs create jobs for people in the fishing industry and other related businesses. They also
15 supply us with food. Reefs protect our coasts—the coral slows waves down and protects beaches from erosion.

Coral reefs are also popular with divers—many countries benefit from the tourists that they attract. Lastly, chemicals from reef creatures help scientists create new medicines, which help doctors treat different illnesses.

20 _____ Coral reefs are very important, yet we don't take good care of them. Environmental problems have already killed about twenty percent of the world's reefs. About half of the remaining reefs are dying, and experts believe all of Earth's coral reefs will be in danger by 2050.

Why are the reefs in such trouble? For one thing, people catch too many reef fish
25 and often damage the reefs—divers sometimes break off pieces of coral. Many people make and sell coral jewelry, too.

Polluted water also causes problems because reef-destroying algae grow in dirty water. Even air pollution hurts coral reefs. Global warming causes warmer ocean water, which can cause polyps to lose helpful algae. Without that algae, coral turns
30 white. This is called "bleaching," and if it continues, the coral dies.

_____ Can we save coral reefs? Experts say yes—if we make hard choices. Many people around the world are working to protect reefs, but we need to do more. More than 100 countries have created marine protected areas, where fishing is limited or even banned. Another important step is fighting pollution.

35 Humans and coral polyps are very different, but we both build amazing cities. We will both benefit if people protect our beautiful oceans.

Comprehension

A Answer the questions about *Cities in the Sea*.

1. Purpose The purpose of the article is to _____.

   a. show how to protect coral reefs

   b. explain why coral reefs are important

   c. tell readers about the Great Barrier Reef

2. Vocabulary A "habitat" is a place where _____. (line 11)

   a. people fish

   b. animals or plants naturally live

   c. there are few animals or plants

3. Detail Coral reefs help protect coasts by _____.

   a. absorbing pollution

   b. releasing important chemicals

   c. slowing down waves

4. Detail About _____ percent of the world's coral reefs have died.

   a. 20

   b. 50

   c. 80

5. Inference The helpful algae gives coral its _____.

   a. color

   b. hardness

   c. size

B **Complete the word web.** Use the words from the article.

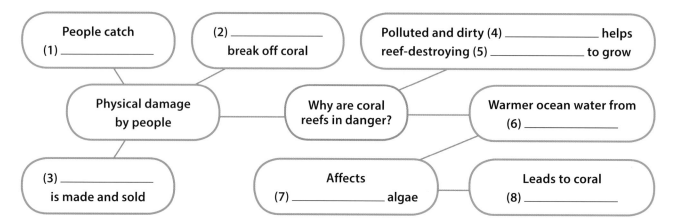

People catch (1) _____

(2) _____ break off coral

Polluted and dirty (4) _____ helps reef-destroying (5) _____ to grow

Physical damage by people

Why are coral reefs in danger?

Warmer ocean water from (6) _____

(3) _____ is made and sold

Affects (7) _____ algae

Leads to coral (8) _____

C **CRITICAL THINKING** **Talk with a partner.** What kinds of "hard choices" do you think we need to make to save the coral reefs?

Writing

Write a formal letter. Persuade a government official to protect the coral reefs.

Send | Forward | Reply | Save | Close | Print | Contacts

To: Benjamin Moore   Subject: Save our reefs

Dear Sir,

I am writing about the state of the coral reefs in our country. We have beautiful reefs near our beaches, but they have suffered a lot of damage recently from fishermen and tourists. I feel that we can protect our coral reefs by . . .

Saving Our Reefs

ABOUT THE VIDEO

Coral reefs are important habitats for many marine animals, and we should protect them.

BEFORE YOU WATCH

Check (✓) the words you think describe coral reefs.

◯ endangered   ◯ a type of marine plant   ◯ mainly found in deep water

◯ colorful   ◯ sensitive to environmental changes

WHILE YOU WATCH

A **Circle the correct answers.**

1. The reef's structure is formed by the (**waste / outer skeletons**) of the polyps.

2. A bleaching event occurs when the water becomes too (**warm / cold**).

3. Marine plants use carbon dioxide to (**make food / breathe**).

B **Watch the video again.** Number the sequence of events (**1–5**).

_____ Human activities increase the amount of carbon dioxide in oceans.

_____ Many species could become extinct as a result.

_____ Sea creatures that depend on the tiny animals die.

_____ The water becomes acidic.

_____ The shells and skeletons of tiny sea creatures are destroyed, and the creatures die.

AFTER YOU WATCH

Talk with a partner. Would you want to go diving to see coral reefs? In which areas in the world are coral reefs mainly found?

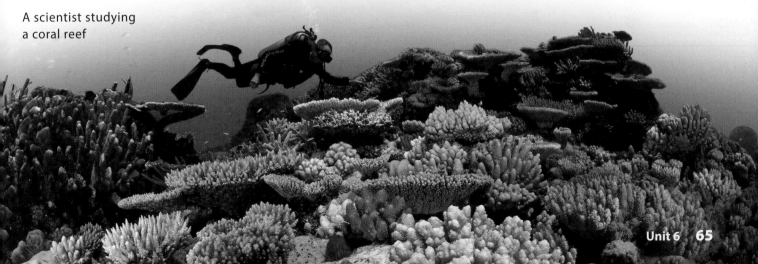

A scientist studying a coral reef

IT MIGHT HAVE BEEN
A TEMPLE.

Preview

A 🎧 2–18 **Listen.** Number the titles in order (**1–3**). One title is extra.

_____ Lost Treasure   _____ An Early Civilization

_____ An Ancient Temple   _____ Mysterious Stones

B 🎧 2–18 **Listen again.** Complete the sentences using the words in the box.

> invaders   statues   religion   treasure   records

1. The _____ on Easter Island could have been used for religious purposes, but there aren't any written _____ from this period to prove it.

2. The Inca king offered gold to the Spanish _____.

3. The Inca _____ might be buried somewhere in the mountains.

4. The temple ruins in Turkey are important because they show that _____ may have come before humans began living in communities.

C **Talk with a partner.** Choose one location and retell the story.

> There might be some lost Inca treasure in the mountains.

> The Spanish captured an Inca king. They . . .

Ruins of a temple in Turkey

Language Focus

A 🎧 2–19 **Listen and read.** Then repeat the conversation and replace the words in blue.

REAL ENGLISH Check this out!

B **Practice with a partner.** Replace any words to make your own conversation.

1 Look what I found **behind the school**.

What is it?

near the playground
on the soccer field

2 I think it's made of stone.

It **could** be an ancient arrowhead.

might
must

3 Cool! It must have been used **to hunt wild animals**.

We should take it to the natural history museum.

to fight other tribes
in fierce battles

4 Hey, Stig! Check this out!

I've been looking for that! I made it in my jewelry-making class.

I lost that the other day.
Where did you get that?

🎧 2–20

DESCRIBING PROBABILITY

	Less Sure	More Sure
Present	The lost treasure **could**/**might** be in a cave. But the treasure **might not** even exist.	It **can't**/**couldn't** be in that cave. It's too high. There are many jewels on this necklace. It **must** be very valuable. No one's ever found it. It **must not** exist.
Past	This house **could**/**might** have belonged to the royal family. However, it **might not** have belonged to an important person at all.	The house is huge, so it **must** have belonged to the royal family. There are bedrooms in the building, so it **couldn't** have been a temple.

68 Unit 7

1. Mary: This ruin used to be a huge building. What do you think it was used for?

   Greg: I don't know. It 1. (**might have been / must have been**) a temple. What do you think?

   Mary: No, it 2. (**couldn't have been / might not have been**) a temple because there's one right next to it.

2. Ellen: I have no idea whose notebook this is. It 3. (**might be / must be**) Jessie's.

   Lionel: Oh, here's a photo of a puppy. It 4. (**must have belonged / must belong**) to Laura. She just got a puppy.

3. Alice: Do you think Easter Island's population shrank because of disease?

   Jon: Definitely. Disease 5. (**could have played / must have played**) a big part.

   Alice: Yeah, but maybe there were other reasons, too. For example, some people 6. (**might have left / must have left**) the island because it was getting too crowded.

D **Rewrite the sentences.** Use the words in parentheses.

1. It's possible that the treasure is in a cave. (**could**)
   The treasure could be in a cave.

2. I'm certain that this building is a temple. (**must**)
   _____

3. They definitely got the stone from this valley. (**must**)
   _____

4. It's impossible for this site to contain any artifacts. (**can't**)
   _____

5. It's possible that they didn't leave any written records. (**might not**)
   _____

E 🎧 2–22 **Work in a group.** Listen to the stories of three mysteries and take notes. What do you think happened? Discuss your ideas.

> A weather balloon might have crashed at Roswell.

> Maybe. Or it could have been a secret plane.

A stone ball from Costa Rica

The Real World

Tomb Hunter

Albert Lin is a National Geographic Explorer. He is a modern-day tomb hunter. He's trying to answer one of history's greatest mysteries: Where is the tomb of the Mongol leader Genghis Khan? Ever since he took a backpacking trip to Mongolia, Lin has been searching for the great leader's final resting place.

A 🎧 2-23 **Listen.** Mark each sentence as **F** for Fact or **T** for Theory.

1. Genghis Khan was the leader of a large empire in the 13th century. _____

2. Genghis Khan is buried in the Forbidden Zone. _____

3. The Forbidden Zone is now open to some researchers. _____

4. Genghis Khan was buried with a great deal of treasure. _____

B 🎧 2-24 **Listen.** Check (✓) the techniques Albert Lin uses.

- ⬡ crowdsourcing
- ⬡ digging in the ground
- ⬡ studying satellite images
- ⬡ computer scanning
- ⬡ creating 3-D images
- ⬡ entering underground tombs

CRITICAL THINKING If Genghis Khan's tomb is found, do you think it should be opened? Why or why not?

Pronunciation

Reduction: *have*

A 🎧2–25 **Listen and repeat.**

1. It could have been a hidden treasure.

2. They must have lived in the building.

B 🎧2–26 **Listen.** Complete the sentences.

1. He _____ home already.

2. It _____ an early civilization.

3. They _____ this arrowhead in a battle.

4. This _____ to a king.

5. Jason _____ those things.

6. I _____ my name on my test.

Genghis Khan's portrait can be found on ____ today.

a. the Mongolian flag
b. the Mongolian state symbol
c. Mongolian currency

C **Work with a partner.** Take turns to read the sentences in **B**.

Communication

Solve a puzzle. Work in a group. You are on a quest to find treasure from different civilizations. There are three chests, each containing an item from a certain culture. Each chest is in a different place. Use the clues to complete the chart below.

CULTURES
Aztec, Inca, Maya

ITEMS
mask, cup, bowl

PLACES
mountain, cave, jungle

CLUES

The Maya chest is one number smaller than the Inca chest.

The Aztec chest can't be Chest 1, but must contain the cup.

Chest 2 is in a cave.

Chest 1 contains the bowl, but isn't in the jungle.

CHEST	CULTURE	ITEM	PLACE
1			
2			
3			

The Maya chest could be Chest 1 or 2.

Reading

A **Look at the title and the photo.** What do you know about the Maya? When and where did they live?

B **Skim the article.** What did archaeologists use to think happened to the Maya? What do they think now?

C **Talk with a partner.** What other ancient civilizations do you know?

Mayan temple ruins in Tikal, Guatemala

MAYA MYSTERY

by Guy Gugliotta, writing for National Geographic

🎧 2–27

A lost world is hidden in the rain forests of Central America. There, the Maya built incredible cities. The Maya civilization was at its peak for 750 years, but about 1,000 years ago, the cities were abandoned. Today, the cities are empty. Trees and plants cover the old buildings, and many temples are now ruins. What happened? Why did the Maya leave their
5 beautiful cities?

For years, archaeologists thought that a disaster, like a volcano or an earthquake, must have hit the Maya. Diseases, which were brought by invaders, might have spread through the population. However, researchers now think the Maya had a lot of different problems. One was that the population was probably too big, which must have put too much pressure on
10 the environment.

To understand what happened to the Maya, National Geographic sent me to Central America. I visited Maya cities and talked to the archaeologists who are studying them.

One hot day, I stood next to a river near the ruins of Cancuén. It used to be a great city, but everything changed 1,200 years ago. Invaders came suddenly—probably by boat. I
15 pictured them as I looked at the river. In my mind, I saw the invaders fighting the soldiers first at the river and then in the town.

I followed the path that the invaders must have taken, which led to the ruins of a large red pool. The pool once provided drinking water for the city. Then it became a tomb. The invaders killed the city's leaders and threw their bodies into the water. They killed the king
20 and queen, too, and buried them nearby.

The invaders then left, taking nothing of value. No one knows who they were, what they wanted, or where they went. The city's population must have been scared because they escaped into the rain forest.

The fall of Cancuén was sudden and terrifying. Since then, the reason for the city's strange
25 end has been a mystery to archaeologists.

I learned a different story in Tikal—one of the greatest Maya cities. 1,300 years ago, about 55,000 people lived there. The city had about 3,000 major buildings. But, like Cancuén, its people left.

Archaeologists think Tikal might have had a drought, which would have made it hard to
30 grow food. War with neighboring cities might also have made Tikal weak. The Maya believed that their leaders were gods, so when the king couldn't bring rain or protect them, people started to question his power. Their community might then have fallen apart.

Walking among the temples at Tikal, I imagined the people living there in the city's last days. I could picture them hungry, tired, and scared. Like the Maya in Cancuén, they left
35 behind a great city and a great mystery.

Comprehension

A **Answer the questions about *Maya Mystery*.**

1. Main Idea What is the mystery in the title?

    a. Why did the Maya civilization disappear?

    b. Who were the Maya people?

    c. Where did the Maya hide their treasure?

2. Inference The archaeologists thought the Maya probably died from a disaster or disease because _____.

    a. their deaths were sudden

    b. the Maya had a lot of enemies

    c. they were bad at farming

3. Detail Why did invaders attack Cancuén?

    a. to take their treasure

    b. to kill the king

    c. No one knows.

4. Vocabulary The word "drought" means a period of time without any _____. (line 29)

    a. workers

    b. rain

    c. sun

5. Detail What is known to be true about Cancuén but not Tikal?

    a. Its people left the city.

    b. Its people believed in gods.

    c. Its king and queen were killed.

B **Read the sentences below.** Mark each one as **F** for Fact or **T** for Theory.

1. The Maya civilization was at its peak for about 750 years. _____

2. The Maya population shrank because of a natural disaster. _____

3. The city of Cancuén was abandoned 1,200 years ago. _____

4. The people who invaded Cancuén came by boat. _____

5. Tikal had a drought, which made it hard to grow food. _____

6. War with neighboring cities made Tikal weak. _____

7. The Maya believed that their leaders were gods. _____

C **Talk with a partner.** Which mystery in this unit would you like to help solve? Why?

Writing

Write a short essay. Describe a mystery you know.

Crop Formations

Every year, mysterious crop circles or formations appear in fields in England. Some people think aliens might have made them. Others think that people made them as a prank . . .

Tutankhamun

ABOUT THE VIDEO

Scientists are trying to solve the mystery of Tutankhamun's death.

BEFORE YOU WATCH

Circle the correct answers. What do you know about Tutankhamun?

1. Tutankhamun became King of Egypt when he was (**9** / **17**) years old.

2. Tutankhamun was (**18** / **28**) when he died.

3. Tutankhamun died around (**300** / **3,000**) years ago.

WHILE YOU WATCH

A Check your answers to the Before You Watch questions.

B Watch the video again. Check (✓) the three possible theories for King Tut's death that are mentioned in the video.

1. He might have been bitten by a snake. ⬭

2. He could have been killed during a battle. ⬭

3. He might have died as a result of a hunting accident. ⬭

4. He might have had a terrible illness. ⬭

5. He could have been murdered. ⬭

6. He could have died in a fire. ⬭

AFTER YOU WATCH

Talk with a partner. Which theory did the scientists in the video think was most likely? Do you think the evidence was strong?

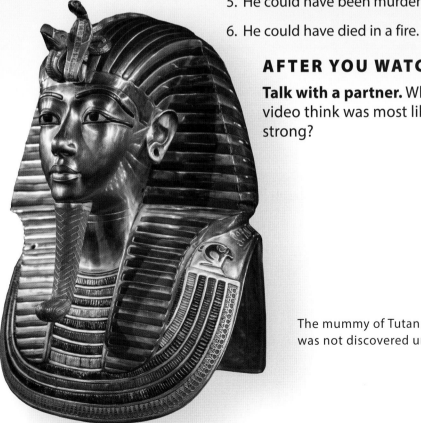

The mummy of Tutankhamun was not discovered until 1922.

IT'S TALLER THAN THE EIFFEL TOWER!

The minute hand of the Mecca clock is 22 meters long.

Preview

A 🎧2–28 **Listen.** Complete the sentences using the correct forms of the words in the box.

> long   interesting   tall   deep   large

1. Arsenalna Station is the _____ metro station in the world.

2. The Seikan Tunnel is the _____ and deepest underground rail tunnel.

3. The Gherkin is one of the _____ buildings in London.

4. The *Oasis of the Seas* is the _____ cruise ship in the world.

5. The Abraj Al-Bait Towers has the world's _____ clock tower.

B 🎧2–28 **Listen again.** Circle the correct answers.

1. At about (**105** / **205**) meters deep, Arsenalna Station is too deep to reach on a single escalator.

2. Almost half of the Seikan Tunnel runs (**through mountains** / **under the sea**).

3. The 16th floor of The Gherkin is the (**largest** / **most interesting**).

4. The *Oasis of the Seas* is just as (**long** / **tall**) as its sister ship, the *Allure*.

5. The Abraj Al-Bait Towers is (**shorter** / **taller**) than Shanghai Tower.

C **Talk with a partner.** What is the most impressive man-made structure in your country? What do you know about it?

> There's a new skyscraper downtown that's really tall.

> I think it's the tallest in the city.

The Gherkin is 180 meters tall.

Language Focus

A 🎧 2–29 **Listen and read.** Then repeat the conversation and replace the words in blue.

B **Practice with a partner.** Replace any words to make your own conversation.

🎧 2–30

DESCRIBING AND COMPARING THINGS

You can't get to Arsenalna Station on a single escalator. It's **too deep**.

Celia is **old enough** to drive. She's twenty-one.

The *Oasis of the Seas* is just **as tall as** the *Allure of the Seas*.

The Mecca Clock Tower is **taller than** Taipei 101. It's also **newer**.

The Empire State Building was **more expensive than** The Gherkin to build.

The Seikan Tunnel is **the longest** undersea tunnel in the world. It's also **the deepest**.

The Burj Khalifa is **the most famous** skyscraper in Dubai.

C 🎧 2–31 **Complete the sentences.** Use the words in the box with *too* or *enough*. Then listen and check your answers.

> expensive   hungry   slow   old   tall   wide

1. I can't afford the ticket price to the observation deck. It's _____.

2. Jay is 15. He isn't _____ to drive yet.

3. Six cars can't drive side by side on that bridge. It's not _____.

4. This train is _____. We'll never get to the movie theater in time.

5. I'm not _____ to reach the shelf. Can you help me?

6. Sorry, but I already ate. I was _____ to wait for you!

D **Complete the sentences.** Use the correct forms of the words in parentheses.

(1) ___The most memorable___ (**memorable**) way to see New York City is from one of its many skyscrapers. (2) _____ (**famous**) is surely the Empire State Building. But some visitors who have gone to Top of the Rock at Rockefeller Center say the view from there is just as good as the view from the Empire State Building. Others even claim that the view is actually (3) _____ (**good**) in the whole city. Tickets, however, are just (4) _____ (**expensive**) those at the Empire State Building. But Top of the Rock's lines are shorter, and its elevator is (5) _____ (**fast**). So while Top of the Rock is not (6) _____ (**famous**) the Empire State Building, it's attracting more and more tourists.

E **Work in a group.** Pick one structure below and compare it to something else. Add your own ideas. Take turns.

> The Eiffel Tower   The Great Wall of China   Machu Picchu
> The Great Pyramid   The Leaning Tower of Pisa   The White House

> The Great Pyramid is the largest pyramid in Egypt. I think it's a more interesting place to visit than the Eiffel Tower because . . .

Earthscraper

As cities get bigger and bigger, the traditional solution has been to build skyscrapers. But architects in Mexico City—one of the world's largest cities—have another idea. Instead of building up, they want to build down. If this building gets built, it will be the world's first earthscraper.

A 🎧2-32 **Listen.** Complete the chart with information about Earthscraper.

Number of stories	
Depth	
Reason for building	
Location in city	

B 🎧2-32 **Listen again.** Circle **T** for True or **F** for False.

1. Earthscraper will be taller than the Eiffel Tower.   **T**   **F**

2. Earthscraper has a glass top to allow sunlight in.   **T**   **F**

3. The museum will showcase cultures around the world.   **T**   **F**

4. Earth lobbies will help to make the air in the building better.   **T**   **F**

CRITICAL THINKING   Do you think Earthscraper will be built someday? Would you like to live in a building like this?

Pronunciation

Emphatic stress

A 🎧 2-33 **Listen and repeat.**

1. The new plane is **much** faster than the previous model.

2. The Twister roller coaster is **way** too scary for me!

3. The new bridge is **just** as long as the old one.

B 🎧 2-34 **Listen.** Underline the stressed words.

1. The view from here is a lot better than I thought.

2. The price of the high-speed train is way too expensive.

3. The new stadium is a little easier to get to.

4. I told you this bridge is just as long as the City Bridge.

5. The car we rented was not nearly big enough for all of us.

6. The seats on the new ferry are so much more comfortable.

C **Work with a partner.** Take turns to read the sentences in **B**.

DO YOU KNOW?

The first building in the world to have more than 100 floors was ____.

a. the John Hancock Center
b. the Empire State Building
c. Taipei 101

Communication

Create a quiz. Work with a partner. Complete the sentences to create a true/false quiz. Then test your quiz on another pair.

1. _____ is the biggest _____ in the world.

2. _____ is much higher than _____.

3. _____ is not as long as _____.

4. _____ is faster than _____.

5. _____ is farther north than _____.

6. _____ has a smaller population than _____.

7. _____ is the oldest _____.

8. The _____ is too _____ to _____.

9. The most _____ country in the world is _____.

10. _____.

> Châtelet–Les Halles station in Paris is the biggest underground train station in the world. True or false?

Reading

A **Look at the title and the photo.** What do you think the SeaOrbiter is?

B **Scan the article.** What is one thing scientists will be able to do on the SeaOrbiter?

C **Talk with a partner.** Why do you think some people want to build something like the SeaOrbiter?

SEAORBITER

Staring out of your bedroom window, you watch as a great white shark swims by. Soon an octopus comes into view, followed by a jellyfish. You're on the SeaOrbiter, one of the most high-tech vessels ever created for ocean exploration.

5 The 60-meter-tall vessel, which is being built with support from the National Geographic Society, has an unusual design. The top half is above the ocean's surface, while the bottom is underwater. Unlike a ship, the SeaOrbiter is so energy-efficient that it can stay in the water for long periods without returning to land to refuel. "Scientists can observe the
10 oceans for months or even years on end," SeaOrbiter operations director Bill Todd says.

While other vessels make a lot of noise as they move through water, the SeaOrbiter will be quiet. Although the vessel won't make much noise, it will pick up plenty. Super-sensitive underwater recorders will capture
15 sounds from marine life, such as whales that are too far below the vessel to be seen. Check out some of the SeaOrbiter's coolest features:

The Lab An egg-shaped space with three levels, the above-water marine lab will have several aquariums. These will contain small marine animals that scientists can view up close. They can also use the high-tech lab
20 equipment to test pollution levels in seawater.

Power Sources With more than 280 square meters of solar panels on its sides and the wind turbine near the top, the SeaOrbiter will run mostly on solar and wind energy. Its motors will be turned on only when necessary, such as when entering a port. "The vessel is very eco-friendly," Todd says.
25 "Our goal is to study the ocean without changing it."

Divers' Delight The diving equipment room is located seven meters above the ocean. After putting on scuba gear, scientists will be able to take an outdoor elevator and go 12 meters below the water's surface.

Remotely Operated Vehicles Below the surface are Remotely Operated
30 Vehicles, devices that let scientists explore underwater mountains, canyons, and even shipwrecks without leaving the vessel. These vehicles can travel deep into the ocean while sending live video back to the SeaOrbiter.

Life Onboard With room for 22 people, the living area on the SeaOrbiter will be of top quality. Bedrooms will come with TVs, computers, and large
35 underwater windows acting as personal aquariums. There will be several classrooms and even a fitness center.

When the SeaOrbiter is launched, it will sail to remote parts of oceans. It will move with the currents while scientists conduct research. This incredible vessel, says Todd, "will help us uncover the secrets of the sea."

Comprehension

A Answer the questions about *SeaOrbiter*.

1. Main Idea The SeaOrbiter is mainly going to be used as a _____.

   a. research vessel

   b. five-star hotel

   c. high-tech weather station

2. Detail What is not mentioned as an advantage the SeaOrbiter has over a regular ship?

   a. It's quieter.

   b. It's more efficient.

   c. It can move more quickly.

3. Detail The SeaOrbiter gets most of its energy from _____.

   a. the sun and wind

   b. seawater

   c. wind and ocean currents

IDIOM

When something is "smooth sailing," it's _____.

a. moving fast
b. difficult to do
c. progressing well

---

4. Vocabulary A "port" is a place where _____. (line 24)

   a. scientists do research

   b. many marine animals live

   c. ships stop to load or unload

5. Inference Scientists on the SeaOrbiter can probably study an animal 3,000 meters below the vessel by sending _____.

   a. a team of divers with a video camera

   b. a remotely controlled vehicle

   c. a submarine with a diver inside

B **Mark where these places are located on the SeaOrbiter.** Are they above the sea (**A**) or below the sea (**B**)?

_____ sound recorders   _____ the lab   _____ the wind turbine

_____ the dive equipment room   _____ remote-controlled vehicles   _____ bedrooms

C CRITICAL THINKING **Talk with a partner.** Do you think it's important to explore the oceans? What might be challenging about life aboard the SeaOrbiter?

Writing

Create a poster of an interesting man-made structure. Include details about its location, who created it, when it was created, why it's impressive, and how it compares to similar structures.

The Sheraton Huzhou Hot Spring Resort is a hotel in Huzhou, China. It has an interesting shape—it's shaped like a horseshoe. The hotel has nicknames like "horseshoe hotel" and "donut hotel." It was designed by an architect named Ma Yansong . . .

Green Museum

BEFORE YOU WATCH

Talk with a partner. Check (✓) the things you think you can find in the green museum in California.

◯ a rain forest   ◯ an aquarium   ◯ a garden

◯ a coral reef   ◯ a research center   ◯ a flower market

WHILE YOU WATCH

A **Check your answers to the Before You Watch question.**

B **Watch the video again.** Circle the correct answers.

1. The California Academy of Sciences has the (**biggest** / **oldest**) green museum in the world.

2. The climate in the dome is (**cool and dry** / **hot and humid**).

3. The water in the aquarium comes from (**a river** / **the ocean**).

4. The aquarium has the (**deepest** / **widest**) tank for a coral reef in the world.

Visitors in the museum

AFTER YOU WATCH

Talk with a partner. Would you like to visit this museum? What do you think is the most interesting thing about the museum?

HE'S A GREAT DIRECTOR, ISN'T HE?

Director Christopher Nolan filming *The Dark Knight Rises* in New York City

Preview

A Label the words below as positive (P) or negative (N).

_____ overrated   _____ brilliant   _____ unrealistic

_____ dull   _____ gorgeous   _____ superb

B 🎧 3–01 **Listen.** Complete the sentences with the words in **A**.

1. Rachel thinks the special effects in *Interstellar* are amazing, but finds the story _____.

2. Keith says the costumes in *Marie Antoinette* are _____.

3. Sun thinks *Frozen* is _____, but likes the soundtrack.

4. Paul thinks the movie *The Grand Budapest Hotel* has an original story with _____ acting.

5. Natalia says the makeup in *Dawn of the Dead* is _____.

C **Talk with a partner.** Talk about a recent movie you have seen. Share what you liked and didn't like about it.

> I recently saw the new *Avengers* movie. The story was pretty exciting!

> How were the special effects?

Language Focus

A 🎧3-02 **Listen and read.** Then repeat the conversation and replace the words in blue.

B **Practice with a partner.** Replace any words to make your own conversation.

🎧3-03

USING TAG QUESTIONS

Benedict Cumberbatch **is** such a great actor, **isn't he**?	Yes, he is.
There **are** four *Hunger Games* movies, **aren't there**?	Yes, there are.
Maleficent **was** brilliant, **wasn't it**?	Yes, it was.
The soundtrack **doesn't** include any original songs, **does it**?	Actually, it does.
Tobey Maguire **starred** in the *Spider-Man* movies, **didn't he**?	Yes, he did.
You **haven't** seen the new *Star Wars* movie, **have you**?	No, I haven't.
James Cameron **will** make more *Avatar* movies, **won't he**?	Yes, he will.
You **can't** see that movie until you're 18, **can you**?	No, I can't.

C **Complete the tag questions.** Then ask and answer the questions with a partner.

1. 3-D always makes a movie more exciting, <u>doesn't it</u> ?

2. You're a fan of Reese Witherspoon, _____ ?

3. You haven't read any of the *Divergent* books, _____ ?

4. Most romantic comedies are really predictable, _____ ?

5. You don't like action movies, _____ ?

6. You've seen all the *Star Trek* movies, _____ ?

D 🎧3–04 **Complete the conversation.** Then listen and check your answers.

Sam: Do you like the actress Jennifer Lawrence?

Kylie: She was in the *X-Men* movies, (1) _____ ?

Sam: Yes, (2) _____ . And the *Hunger Games* movies.

Kylie: Oh, right. Those made a lot of money, didn't they?

Sam: Yeah, (3) _____ . The movies were really successful.

Kylie: By the way, I'm taking my nephew out for a movie tomorrow. Any suggestions?

Sam: He's still in elementary school, (4) _____ ?

Kylie: No, (5) _____ . He's in middle school now.

Sam: How about an animated movie? He hasn't seen *Big Hero 6* yet, (6) _____ ?

Kylie: I don't think so. Maybe we'll watch that.

E **Work in a group.** Talk about the topics below. Ask follow-up questions.

favorite actors	action movies	pop music
science fiction movies	favorite books	favorite movie characters

You like science fiction movies, don't you?

Of course!

Have you seen *Guardians of the Galaxy*?

Movie Flops

Moviemaking is a risky business. Even a simple movie can cost millions of dollars to make. Actor salaries and special effects all add to a movie's cost. Money is also needed for promotion and advertising. But sometimes, movies don't make their money back.

KEANU REEVES
47 RONIN

A 🎧3-05 **Listen.** Based on the speaker's definition, which of the American movies below are "flops"? Circle the movies.

MOVIE	COST (MILLION)	U.S. TICKET SALES	INTERNATIONAL TICKET SALES
Pacific Rim	$190	$101	$309
R.I.P.D.	$130	$34	$45
Despicable Me 2	$76	$368	$606
47 Ronin	$175	$38	$113

B 🎧3-06 **Listen.** Check (✓) the claims that the speaker makes.

1. One reason a movie can flop is that it gets terrible reviews. ⬜
2. Big-name actors and actresses don't always help make a movie successful. ⬜
3. Movie studios make sequels and remakes because they aren't creative. ⬜
4. Hollywood is very careful when it selects which movies to make. ⬜

Discussion. Do you know any movie that didn't do well? Do you think it was a flop?

Pronunciation
Intonation in tag questions

A 🎧3-07 **Listen and repeat.**

1. The *Harry Potter* movies made a lot of money, didn't they? (asking for agreement)

2. You haven't seen all the *Harry Potter* movies, have you? (asking for information)

B 🎧3-08 **Listen.** Are the speakers asking for agreement (**A**) or information (**I**)? Write the letters.

1. That film festival was awesome, wasn't it? _____

2. *Planet of the Apes* has been remade twice, hasn't it? _____

3. You're a big anime fan, aren't you? _____

4. *The Hobbit* trilogy won a lot of awards, didn't it? _____

5. You don't like watching movies in 3-D, do you? _____

6. Movie tickets are so expensive nowadays, aren't they? _____

C **Work with a partner.** Take turns to read the sentences in **B**.

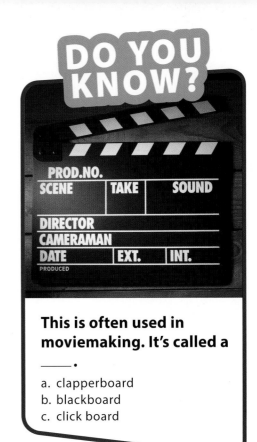

DO YOU KNOW?

This is often used in moviemaking. It's called a

_____.

a. clapperboard
b. blackboard
c. click board

Communication

Play a guessing game. Work with a partner. Think of a movie, an actor/actress, and a TV show. Then write clues for each category below. Read your clues to another pair and get them to guess the answers.

Movie	Actor/Actress	TV Show

This movie came out in 2015. It's part of a movie franchise. It stars Arnold Schwarzenegger.

Oh, I know! It's *Terminator Genisys*, isn't it?

That's right!

Reading

(A) Predict. Which question do you think the article answers?

   a. Are horror movies less scary than they used to be?

   b. Why do people go to horror movies?

   c. What horror movies are most popular?

(B) Scan the article. Circle the three components of horror movies.

(C) Talk with a partner. Do you like horror movies? Why do you think they are so popular?

OUR ATTRACTION to FRIGHT

🎧 3–09

Do you enjoy watching horror movies? Many people do, and scientists are interested in finding out why.

Millions of years of human evolution have made us afraid of certain things. For example, we are afraid of the dark for good reason—sometimes, wild animals or
5   other dangers hid in the dark. In a way, fear has helped humans avoid danger and helped us survive.

Scientists have identified an area of the brain that is linked to fear—the amygdala. This area of the brain produces stronger responses when people view images of animals—as compared to images of people, places, or things. This is
10 strange because animals are not very likely to cause us harm in today's modern world. But perhaps it's the reason why many scary movies have images of animal-like monsters. However, brain scan research also shows that horror movies don't actually create fear responses in the amygdala. This makes researchers curious to know the kind of emotions people are really feeling when
15 they watch a horror movie.

It's important to understand what creates horror in movies. Psychologist Glenn D. Walters has identified three factors. One is tension, created through mystery, terror, shock, and mood. The second is relevance, which can be fears we all have, such as fear of the unknown, or death. The third factor is unrealism. In one
20 research study, students were shown horrible images from documentary movies. Most couldn't watch them. But these same students paid money to see even worse images in horror movies. Why? They knew the movie was not real. This may explain why documentary-style movies that are presented as "real"— such as *Paranormal Activity*—are seen as particularly frightening.

25 The attraction to fear is intriguing on a psychological level. Many theories have tried to explain its appeal. One suggests that young people like horror movies because adults frown upon them. For adults, the appeal may be a sort of dark curiosity, similar to what happens when we stop to look at a car accident. Another theory says that we enjoy horror because of the feeling of confidence
30 we experience afterward.

Although many theories have been suggested, we still don't fully understand our fascination with horror movies. But whatever reasons people have for watching horror, one thing is clear—this movie genre is not going anywhere.

Comprehension

A Answer the questions about *Our Attraction to Fright*.

1. Purpose The purpose of the second paragraph is to explain _____.

    a. what horror movies are

    b. why we love horror movies

    c. why we fear some things

2. Inference Horror movies often make use of music to add to the _____.

    a. unrealism

    b. tension

    c. relevance

3. Detail It's easier for people to watch scary images in movies than in documentaries because they know that the images _____.

    a. aren't real

    b. aren't of people

    c. aren't as scary

4. Vocabulary In line 27, "frown upon" means _____.

    a. to be unafraid of

    b. to show disapproval of

    c. to refuse to see

5. Cohesion The sentence "It makes us feel better about ourselves because we made it through the horror safely" would go best at the end of the _____ paragraph.

    a. third

    b. fourth

    c. fifth

B **Read the sentences below.** Mark them as **T** for True, **F** for False, or **NG** for Not Given.

1. There are evolutionary reasons why we fear certain things. _____

2. The amygdala responds more strongly to objects than to landmarks. NG

3. Scary movies activate fear responses in the amygdala. _____

4. Students spend a lot of money watching horror movies. _____

5. Documentary-style horror movies are especially scary because they feel real. _____

6. People in their 20s watch more horror movies than anyone else. _____

C **CRITICAL THINKING** **Talk with a partner.** Do you think watching horror movies is harmful in any way?

Writing

Write a movie review. Describe the movie and share what you liked or didn't like about it.

MOVIE REVIEW FORUM

Heartwarming Story ★★★★☆

I watched *Chappie* recently. The movie is about a robot who can think and feel like a normal human. The movie characters were very interesting and funny. The story was brilliant. It made me think about issues in our society. I would definitely recommend this to everyone because . . .

Walk of Fame

ABOUT THE VIDEO

The Hollywood Walk of Fame is a famous sidewalk in California, U.S.A.

BEFORE YOU WATCH

What do you know about the Hollywood Walk of Fame? Circle **T** for True or **F** for False.

1. Most of the people on the Walk of Fame are movie stars.   **T   F**

2. There are some fictional characters on the Walk of Fame.   **T   F**

3. The first stars are over 100 years old.   **T   F**

WHILE YOU WATCH

A Check your answers to the Before You Watch questions.

B Watch the video again. Circle the correct answers.

1. (**One / Neither**) of the speakers has been to Hollywood.

2. In the video, George Clooney is making his (**handprints / footprints**) in the concrete.

3. The speakers (**liked / didn't like**) the last *Harry Potter* movie.

4. The female speaker (**is / isn't**) interested in celebrities.

AFTER YOU WATCH

Talk with a partner. Are you interested in celebrities? Is there a place in your country that's similar to the Walk of Fame?

The Hollywood Walk of Fame

I WISH I COULD BE AN **ATHLETE!**

A competitor at the
Sandboarding World
Championship in Germany

Preview

A 🎧 3–10 **Listen to the conversation.** Number the wishes (**1–5**).

___ play the piano well   ___ cure diseases   ___ be a talented architect

___ travel back in time   ___ be an athlete

B 🎧 3–10 **Listen again.** What would the people do if their wishes came true? Match.

1. John   ○   ○ a. would design interesting buildings

2. Christopher ○   ○ b. would like to meet Einstein

3. Mariko   ○   ○ c. would find a cure for cancer

4. Luke   ○   ○ d. would set an Olympic record

5. Sara   ○   ○ e. would perform in concerts around the world

C **Talk with a partner.** Look at the wishes in **A**. Which wish would you choose? Why?

> I wish I could travel back in time. That way, I could find the answers to ancient mysteries!

> Which period would you go back to?

Language Focus

A 🎧 3–11 **Listen and read.** Then repeat the conversation and replace the words in blue.

REAL ENGLISH Do you mean . . . ?

B **Practice with a partner.** Replace any words to make your own conversation.

1
Do you ever wish you had a superpower?

Do you mean like being able to **fly**?

Yeah, what do you wish you could do?

see through walls
travel back in time

2
I wish I could **breathe underwater**.

make myself invisible
predict the future

3
What power would you **want**?

I'd want to control people's minds.

like
wish for

4
Why?

If I could do that, I could make **all my teachers give me A's**!

everyone do what I say
people do my chores

🎧 3–12

TALKING ABOUT WISHES AND IMAGINARY SITUATIONS

I **wish** I **were** rich and famous.
I **wish** I **didn't have** so much homework.
I **wish** I **could speak** every language well.

If you **were** rich, **would** you **use** the money to travel?	Yes, I **would**. I'**d use** it to go to Antarctica. No, I **wouldn't**. I'**d use** it to help people.
If you **could have** any superpower, what power **would** you **want** to have?	I'**d want** to be able to fly.
Where **would** you **go if** you **could go** anywhere in the world?	I'**d go** to Australia and New Zealand.

C 🎧 3–13 **Complete the conversations.** Use the correct forms of the words in parentheses. Then listen and check your answers.

1. Kay: What would you do if you (1) _____ (**be**) rich?

   Hugh: I (2) _____ (**buy**) a house for my parents.

2. Alfred: If you (3) _____ (**can have**) any superpower, what superpower

   (4) _____ you _____ (**want**)?

   Sandy: I think I'd want to be able to read people's minds.

3. Erin: If you (5) _____ (**can live**) forever, would you be happy?

   Roger: No way. I (6) _____ (**not want**) that.

4. Trevor: If you (7) _____ (**not have to**) go to school, how different would your life be?

   Nancy: It (8) _____ (**not be**) different at all. I'd still go to school.

D **Complete the sentences.** Use the correct forms of the phrases in the box.

be taller	be more hours in a day	~~can go back in time~~
can sing well	have fewer words	put in more effort

1. I wish I _could go back in time_. It would be interesting to meet Abraham Lincoln.

2. I'm too short to join the basketball team. I wish I _____.

3. I never have enough time to see my friends. I wish there _____.

4. I wish English _____. There are too many to remember!

5. I wish I _____. It would be fun to enter a talent competition.

6. Climate change is a real problem. I wish people _____ to find a solution.

E **Work in a group.** Imagine you had three wishes. What are they? Share your wishes with your group members.

> I wish I could talk to animals.

> Why?

> I'd like to know what they think of us.

The Real World

Power of a
Wish

The **Make-A-Wish Foundation**
is an organization that grants
wishes to sick children aged 3
to 18. It has been granting
wishes for more than 30 years.

**Chris Saling
with Joel Sartore**

A 🎧 **3–14** **Listen.** Circle the correct answers.

In 1980, a boy named Chris Greicius was dying from 1. (**cancer** / **a heart disease**). His wish
was to be a 2. (**firefighter** / **police officer**). A few officers from Arizona, U.S.A., heard about
his wish, and they wanted to help. Within a few days, they 3. (**made his wish come true** /
raised a sum of money). After this experience, two of the officers decided that they
wanted to help children 4. (**from poor families** / **with life-threatening illnesses**). So they
created the Make-A-Wish Foundation. Today, the organization has granted more than
300,000 wishes to children 5. (**around the world** / **in the United States**).

B 🎧 **3–15** **Listen.** Circle **T** for True or **F** for False.

1. Saling's wish was to go on a photo shoot with Joel Sartore.	T	F
2. Saling took photos of wild animals.	T	F
3. National Geographic held an exhibition to display Saling's photos.	T	F
4. Saling started to raise money to support medical research on his condition.	T	F

CRITICAL THINKING   If you had some money to give to charity, whom would you give it to?
Do you know any other organizations that help children?

Pronunciation
Contractions: *'ll* and *'d*

A 🎧 3-16 **Listen and repeat.**

1. I'll buy a new car. 2. I'd buy a new car.

B 🎧 3-17 **Listen.** Circle the sounds you hear.

1. 'll   'd   2. 'll   'd   3. 'll   'd
4. 'll   'd   5. 'll   'd   6. 'll   'd

C **Work with a partner.** Take turns to read the sentences below.

1. If I could visit any city for a day, I'd go to Barcelona.

2. I'll practice the piano after school today.

3. If the weather is nice this weekend, I'll go for a picnic at the beach.

4. If I could meet anyone in the world, I'd want to meet Beyoncé.

DO YOU KNOW?

People often throw ____ into a fountain to make a wish.
a. flowers
b. pebbles
c. coins

Communication

Play a game. Work with a partner. Read the questions below. Guess what your partner's answers will be. Then check your guesses and ask follow-up questions.

Questions	My guesses	My partner's answers
If you could be the size of a building or an insect, which would you be?		
Which would you choose to spend one day as—a cat or a bird?		
If you could be very rich or very good-looking, which would you choose?		
If you had to give up pizza or burgers, which would you never eat again?		
If you could bend metal or see through walls, which would you pick?		
If you had to lose your hearing or your sense of taste, which would it be?		
If you could be a language or musical genius, which would you be?		

If you could be the size of a building or an insect, which would you be?

I'd be the size of an insect.

Oh, I didn't guess that correctly. Why would you want to be so small?

Kelvin Doe

Reading

A **Talk with a partner.** Who are some young people who have made a difference in the world? What did they do?

B **Scan the article.** Where are the teenagers from?

C **Skim the article.** Place the headings in the correct places. One is extra.

a. The Journalist   b. The Musician

c. The Inventor   d. The App Developer

Rene Silva

MAKING A DIFFERENCE 🎧 3–18

_____ Kelvin Doe was born during Sierra Leone's civil war. He was six when the war ended. Today, he represents how this West African country is moving forward. A short film about him has already gathered a few million views on YouTube.

Kelvin is a self-taught engineer. At age 11, he began digging through trash to find
5 electronic parts to create things. Since then, he has built a battery, a generator to provide electricity in his neighborhood, and a radio station from recycled materials.

At age 15, he won a competition that took him to the United States. There, he spoke about his inventions to students at the Massachusetts Institute of Technology (MIT). He also appeared on CNN and NBC News, and was a speaker at TEDxTeen. He has
10 helped inspire and educate people through these events.

_____ Zea Tongeman, a teenager from the United Kingdom, never thought of herself as a tech person. "I used to think technology was just fixing computers," Zea says. But one day she participated in a technology workshop at her school. A fashion designer came and showed the class how technology helps her create unique designs.

15 "This was really what got me excited about technology," Zea says, "because it showed me that you don't have to be sitting at a computer screen all day typing really fast. You can be creative with it."

She also found that technology can educate people. With a friend, she designed an app called Jazzy Recycling. It aims to get people to recycle by making the task into a
20 game. The app helps users find recycling locations and shows them what to recycle. They can then scan, share, and get rewards through the app.

_____ Like many Brazilian teenagers, Rene Silva is interested in computer games, soccer, and music, but he also has another interest. He wants people to understand what the poor neighborhoods, or _favelas_, are really like. Many people see Rio de
25 Janeiro's _favelas_ only as dangerous places—places to avoid. Rene has used social media to show a more positive side.

When Rene was 11, a teacher suggested he set up a neighborhood newspaper. He worked hard writing reports for the newspaper. At 17, he became famous for tweeting about a police raid. On his blog, he corrected mistakes made by TV reporters. Soon,
30 his followers increased from a few hundred to tens of thousands.

At age 19, he wrote his first book about the _favelas_. He hopes that it will help educate others about the people there. "Today," Rene says, "there is more recognition of the people who are trying to do good and change the reality of the place where they live."

Comprehension

A Answer the questions about *Making a Difference*.

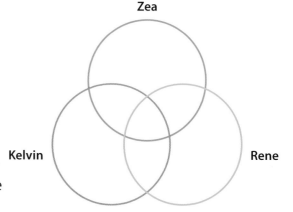

IDIOM

If something is "beyond your wildest dreams," it's ____ than you imagined.

a. worse
b. better

1. Cohesion The sentence "Many young people in Sierra Leone now want to be like Kelvin" would go best at the end of the ____ paragraph.

   a. first   b. second   c. third

2. Detail Zea changed her mind about technology when she saw how ____.

   a. easy it was to use

   b. creative she could be with it

   c. an app could affect people

3. Inference The Jazzy Recycling app gets people to recycle by ____.

   a. making the task fun

   b. giving them cash

   c. teaching them about the environment

4. Detail Rene is trying to educate people about ____.

   a. life in *favelas*

   b. news reporting in Brazil

   c. using social media

5. Vocabulary In line 32, "recognition" means ____.

   a. cooperation

   b. reward

   c. acknowledgment

B **Complete the Venn diagram.** Write the letters of the descriptions in the correct places.

a. wrote a book

b. won a competition

c. is involved in recycling

d. wrote for a newspaper

e. designs apps

f. was inspired by a fashion designer

g. is using his or her influence to educate people

Zea

Kelvin   Rene

C **CRITICAL THINKING** **Talk with a partner.** How can you make a difference in your community?

Writing

Write an essay. What three changes would you like to see in the world? What do you wish you could do to make these changes?

Home   **BLOG**   Photos   Contact   About Me

One of my wishes is to see every child being able to go to school. I feel that education is very important for learning about ourselves and the world. If I were in the government, I would make it possible for poor children to receive an education by . . .

RoboBees

ABOUT THE VIDEO

Robert Wood is a National Geographic Explorer. He is building unique robots to help people.

BEFORE YOU WATCH

What do you think the robot insects are like? Check (✓) the features.

- ◯ tiny
- ◯ soft
- ◯ cheap to make
- ◯ can fly
- ◯ can lift heavy things
- ◯ built from recycled materials

WHILE YOU WATCH

A Check your answers to the Before You Watch question.

B Watch the video again. Complete the sentences.

1. Wood hopes his robots will be useful in _____.

   a. monitoring people's health   b. exploring space and oceans

2. Wood's team gets ideas from _____.

   a. nature   b. machines

3. In the next _____ years, Wood believes his robots will be able to help people do dangerous tasks.

   a. 5   b. 20

4. Wood is creating robots that _____ bees.

   a. work in groups like   b. are as intelligent as

AFTER YOU WATCH

Talk with a partner. If you could build a robot, what kind of robot would you want to build? Do you think robots are important to humans?

A robot created by Wood and his team

WHAT WOULD YOU DO?

Preview

A 🎧 **3–19** **Listen.** What situations are the people facing? Circle the correct answers in the first column.

SITUATION	FRIEND'S ADVICE
1. Susan saw someone (**stealing** / **cheating**).	
2. Matt's neighbors refused to (**turn down their music** / **clear their trash**).	
3. May (**dirtied** / **damaged**) something in a store.	
4. Robert found a (**handbag** / **wallet**) on the sidewalk.	

B 🎧 **3–20** **Listen.** What is their friend's advice? Complete the second column in **A**.

C **Talk with a partner.** What would you do in each situation in **A**?

> I'd say something to the classmate.

> I probably wouldn't do anything.

What would you do if you saw
someone being pickpocketed?

Language Focus

A 🎧 3–21 **Listen and read.** Then repeat the conversation and replace the words in blue.

B **Practice with a partner.** Replace any words to make your own conversation.

🎧 3–22

LANGUAGE REVIEW

Describing actions that continue to the present	**Describing probability**
She's **been waiting** here for an hour.	This bag **could**/**might** belong to a man.
They'**ve been playing** music since two o'clock.	That **can't**/**couldn't** be his car. His car isn't black.
	He **could**/**might** have taken the wallet.
Passive form	I **must** have left my homework at home.
My neighbor **was taken** to the hospital.	She **couldn't** have left the book there. She was
Most crimes **are reported by** regular people.	holding it just now.
Giving advice	**Talking about imaginary situations**
You **should apologize** for saying that.	If I **saw** a crime, I'**d call** the police.
You **could ask** the teacher for some advice.	If I **had** enough money, I'**d buy** a new computer.

C 🎧 3–23 **Circle the correct answers.** Then listen and check.

1. Amy: If you had an extra $1,000, what 1. (**would** / **must**) you do with it?

   Louis: That's a lot of money. 2. (**I'd** / **I'll**) buy a new computer. 3. (**I was using** / **I've been using**) this one for five years.

2. Chris: I heard the answers to today's test 4. (**were being stolen** / **were stolen**). They 5. (**took** / **were taken**) off Mr. Lee's desk when he left to make a call.

   Kelly: It 6. (**should** / **must**) be someone in our class. But who 7. (**would** / **should**) do something like that?

3. Peter: Do you know whose backpack this is?

   Tania: It 8. (**should** / **might**) be Jennifer's. She has a blue bag.

   Peter: No, it 9. (**can't be** / **might not have been**) hers. Look—the initials "T. R." are on it.

D **Complete the sentences.** Use your own ideas.

1. I don't see him anywhere. He must have ___gone home_____ .

2. If you broke your friend's laptop, I think you should _____ .

3. You could _____ after school.

4. They couldn't have _____ . They've been here all morning.

5. James must have been _____ when we were in class.

E **Work in a group.** Talk about what you would do in each situation below.

> A teacher gave you an A+ by mistake.
>
> You saw someone littering.
>
> Someone spread a false rumor about you.
>
> You accidentally broke a vase in a shop.
>
> You were given a flower by a stranger.
>
> Someone fell asleep against you on a bus.

What would you do if someone fell asleep against you on a bus?

I'd wake the person up.

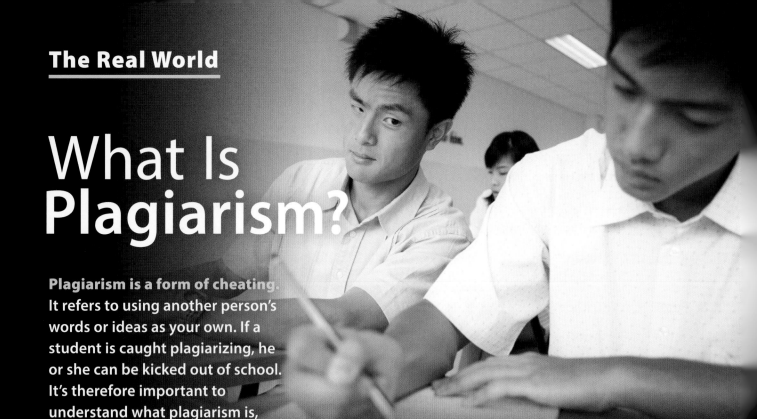

The Real World

What Is Plagiarism?

Plagiarism is a form of cheating. It refers to using another person's words or ideas as your own. If a student is caught plagiarizing, he or she can be kicked out of school. It's therefore important to understand what plagiarism is, and how to avoid it.

A 🎧 3–24 **Listen.** Read each situation below. Write **P** if it's an example of plagiarism.

1. Kevin copied his friend's essay and turned it in as his own. _____

2. Tara put quotation marks around a famous quote and listed the source. _____

3. Zac summarized an author's ideas for his paper and listed the source. _____

4. Pam copied and pasted a paragraph from an online encyclopedia for her report. _____

5. Hee-jin wrote the date of the invention of the light bulb without listing its source. _____

B 🎧 3–25 **Listen.** Complete the notes. Two words are extra.

> cite   summarize   paraphrase   multiple   instructions   list

1. Learn to _____.

2. Use _____ sources.

3. _____ your sources.

4. _____ the source if the origin of the idea is unclear.

CRITICAL THINKING What would you do if you knew a student turned in someone else's essay as his or her own? Why?

Pronunciation
Final *t* or *d* with initial *y*

A 🎧 3-26 **Listen and repeat.**

1. I want you to be honest.   2. What would you do?

B 🎧 3-27 **Listen. Complete the sentences.**

1. How _____ explain the situation?

2. I don't _____ to be angry.

3. _____ like to play a game?

4. Why won't the teacher _____ leave early?

5. I _____ something in my art class.

6. I _____ the email yesterday.

C **Work with a partner.** Take turns to read the sentences in **B**.

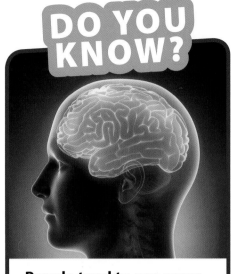

DO YOU KNOW?

People tend to use areas of the brain related to _____ when making moral decisions.
a. emotion
b. logic

Communication

Debate an issue. A large area of forested land on the edge of town has been set aside for a new mall. Some people in the community are for the project, but some aren't. Work in groups of four. Two students are Team A, and two students are Team B. **Team A:** Turn to page 128. **Team B:** Turn to page 132.

> We support this project because we think it will bring many benefits to the town. For example, . . .

Reading

A **Look at the title.** What do you think thought experiments are?

B **Scan the article.** Who designs thought experiments?

C **Read the article.** As you read, think about what you would do in each situation. Share your ideas with a partner.

THOUGHT EXPERIMENTS

🎧 3–28

Like scientists, philosophers use experiments to test their ideas. But unlike scientists, they don't need labs or expensive equipment. Instead, they use moral dilemmas to better understand the human mind. Moral dilemmas are situations where a difficult moral decision has to be made. There are no right or wrong answers to the questions 5 raised by the following thought experiments.

The Runaway Train

You are walking along some train tracks. You look ahead and see five people—they've been tied up and left on the tracks. They're unable to move and are shouting for your help. An out-of-control train is speeding toward them. It's going to hit and kill 10 them if you do nothing.

You see that the train tracks split. A person is crossing the other track, but he doesn't notice the train coming. Next to you is a lever. All you need to do is pull the lever to make the train go onto the other track. If you pull the lever, the train will move onto that track and kill the lone person, but you'll save the five people who are tied up.

15 The Prisoner's Dilemma

You and a friend robbed a bank, but both of you got caught. After being arrested and brought back to the police station, you are placed in two different rooms.

A police officer comes in and makes you the following offer: You can choose to remain silent or confess to the crime. If you confess but your friend does not, you 20 can go free and your friend will go to prison for five years. If you remain silent but your friend confesses, your friend will go free and you'll go to prison for five years. If you both confess, you'll both go to prison for three years. If you both remain silent, the police will charge you with a lesser crime, so both of you will only go to prison for one year.

25 The Famous Pianist

You wake up and find yourself in a hospital bed, covered with tubes. These tubes connect you to a world-famous pianist. The pianist is dying, and only your blood type is suitable for saving him. He'll die if you remove the connection now. If you choose to remain connected for the next nine months, he'll definitely recover. 30 Although you have to stay in bed for nine months, there'll be no danger to your health or life.

What would you do in each of these situations? Philosophers are very interested in studying the different responses people give. They want to find out how people think or react in various situations.

Comprehension

A Answer the questions about *Thought Experiments*.

1. Main Idea   What is true about thought experiments?

   a. They were first created by scientists.

   b. They have a single correct answer.

   c. They are used to test the human mind.

> **IDIOM**
>
> If someone is "between a rock and a hard place," the person is in a situation with _____.
>
> a. unpleasant choices
> b. confusing choices
> c. too many choices

2. Detail   In "The Runaway Train," if you want to let things happen naturally, you'd _____.

   a. get help   b. pull the lever   c. do nothing

3. Vocabulary   Which of the following has a different meaning from the word "lone" in line 14?

   a. lonely   b. solitary   c. single

4. Detail   In "The Prisoner's Dilemma," is it possible for you to avoid prison time?

   a. Yes, if you confess.   b. Yes, if you remain silent.   c. No, it isn't possible.

5. Inference   Thought experiments can be useful for understanding people's _____.

   a. creativity   b. behavior   c. talents

B **Match.** Join each experiment to the question it raises.

1. "The Runaway Train"   ○   ○ a. Should you make personal sacrifices to help someone live?

2. "The Prisoner's Dilemma" ○   ○ b. Do you trust someone enough?

3. "The Famous Pianist"   ○   ○ c. Is killing someone the same as letting them die?

C **CRITICAL THINKING**   **Talk with a partner.** Would your responses to the situations depend on other factors not mentioned in the article? What kind of factors would change your decisions?

Writing

Write a persuasive essay. Your friend is very sick and asks for your help with an important assignment. If you help her, her grade will be higher than usual, which could be unfair to the class. What would you do?

I wouldn't help her. I'd advise her to speak to the teacher to get more time for the assignment. I think it's unfair for me to help her because . . .

Test of Character

BEFORE YOU WATCH

Discuss. In one experiment, people see a thief stealing a woman's bag. What percentage of the people do you think try to help?

WHILE YOU WATCH

A Match each of the people below to their reaction.

1.  2.  3.

a. helps the woman b. watches but does nothing c. runs away

B **Watch the video again.** Complete the summary of the second experiment.

The experiment took place in a restaurant with hidden _____ . An _____ walked past customers and fell to the ground. The lone diner took _____ seconds to help the man. The group of diners took _____ seconds. This is an example of the "Bystander Effect." When people are in a group, they wait for _____ to take control.

AFTER YOU WATCH

Talk with a partner. Do you think the "Bystander Effect" would affect you? Have you ever been in a situation where you needed to help someone?

YOU SHOULD EAT MORE FRUIT!

Preview

A 🎧 3–29 **Listen.** What types of food does the speaker suggest we avoid (x), reduce (↓), or eat a lot of (↑)?

vegetables and fruits _____   whole grains _____   red meat _____

processed food _____   salt and sugar _____   coffee _____

B 🎧 3–29 **Listen again.** Circle **T** for True or **F** for False.

1. Whole grains are healthy because the body breaks them down faster.   **T**   **F**

2. Eating too much red meat can lead to heart disease.   **T**   **F**

3. You should avoid eating foods containing fats.   **T**   **F**

C **Talk with a partner.** What are some healthy foods you like?

> I like eating carrots. They're sweet.

> I love yogurt. I heard that eating it after exercising can help your body recover faster.

An outdoor market in
Otavalo, Ecuador

Language Focus

A 🎧 3–30 **Listen and read.** Then repeat the conversation and replace the words in **blue**.

REAL ENGLISH Any ideas?

B **Practice with a partner.** Replace any words to make your own conversation.

🎧 3–31

LANGUAGE REVIEW

Gerunds

Exercising is a great way to relax.

Drinking less soda can help you lose weight.

Listening to music can improve your mood.

Adding more information

My aunt, **who** studied medicine, always gives good health advice.

Greek yogurt, **which** has a lot of protein, is good for you.

Describing and comparing things

Meat is **cheaper / more expensive** than vegetables.

She's the **fittest / most athletic** person I know.

Vegetables are **(not) as sweet as** fruit.

I'm not going out today. I'm **too tired**.

This coffee is **(not) sweet enough**.

Tag questions

Nuts **are** good for you, **aren't they**?

I **drink** a lot of soda, **don't I**?

She **didn't say** anything, **did she**?

They **can't go** to the party, **can they**?

C 🎧 3–32 **Circle the correct answers.** Then listen and check.

Having a good night's rest feels great, 1. (**does** / **doesn't**) it? 2. (**To get** / **Getting**) the right amount of sleep is important for teens, 3. (**who** / **which**) need energy to play sports or do well on tests. But during the teenage years, there is a reset of the body's internal "clock." This tells a person to fall asleep later and wake up later. Many teens don't get enough sleep because they go to sleep late but get up early for school. School life is busy, and getting through a full day without enough rest isn't as 4. (**easy** / **easier**) as you think. So, if you're feeling 5. (**too tired** / **tired enough**) to give your best during the day, you're probably not getting the eight to nine hours of sleep experts say you need each night.

D **Match.** Join the phrases to make statements. Then talk with a partner. Do you agree or disagree with each statement?

1. Eating too much fatty food ○   ○ a. than a meat-based diet.

2. A vegetarian diet is healthier ○   ○ b. is just as important as a healthy body.

3. Exercising 30 minutes a day ○   ○ c. before and after a workout.

4. It's important to stretch ○   ○ d. who is the best person to give advice.

5. A healthy mind ○   ○ e. can make you sick.

6. If you're unwell, talk to a doctor, ○   ○ f. is long enough to keep yourself fit.

E **Find someone for each of the descriptions below.** Ask questions to find out the information you need.

Find someone who . . .	Name
exercises more than you. plays three different sports. doesn't get enough sleep. has a healthy diet. takes good care of his or her teeth. takes good care of his or her eyes.	

You like to play sports, don't you?

Yeah, I play basketball three times a week.

Oh, I jog once a week.

The Real World

Superfoods

Superfoods have amazing health benefits. Some can help protect you from cancer. Some can lower your blood pressure or help prevent diseases. Plus, they taste great! These so-called "superfoods" can easily be found in your local supermarket.

A 🎧 3-33 **Listen.** Check (✓) the health problems that each superfood may help protect against.

	CANCER	HEART DISEASE	BRAIN DISEASES	HIGH BLOOD PRESSURE
walnuts				
spinach				
avocados				
blueberries				
salmon				

B 🎧 3-33 **Listen again.** Match each food to how the speaker suggests trying it.

1. walnuts ○   ○ a. add to eggs

2. spinach ○   ○ b. eat frozen

3. avocados ○   ○ c. try it raw

4. blueberries ○   ○ d. mix with fruit

5. salmon ○   ○ e. make a smoothie

Discussion. Which of the superfoods above have you tried? What other kinds of foods are good for you?

Pronunciation
Pausing between thought groups

A 🎧 3–34 **Listen and repeat.**

1. A vegetarian diet / is healthier / than a meat-based diet.

2. If you're unwell, / talk to a doctor, / who is the best person / to give advice.

B 🎧 3–35 **Mark the pauses in the sentences with a slash (/).** Then listen and check your answers.

1. A healthy mind is just as important as a healthy body.

2. During the teenage years, there is a reset of the body's internal "clock."

3. These superfoods can be found in your local supermarket.

4. Superfoods may lower your blood pressure, help protect against diabetes, and reduce heart disease risk.

5. Getting the right amount of sleep is important for teens, who need to play sports or do well on tests.

C **Work with a partner.** Take turns to read the sentences in **B**.

DO YOU KNOW?

Which of these foods contains the most vitamin C?

a. oranges
b. bell peppers
c. tomatoes

Communication

Plan a health fair. Work in a group. Prepare a proposal of your ideas.

1. Choose a place for the fair.

2. Brainstorm a list of health topics you want to cover.

3. Plan activities. Include activities for both students and parents.

4. Decide who you will ask to speak at the fair.

5. Choose what food and drink you will serve at the fair.

> We could have the fair in the cafeteria.

> The cafeteria isn't big enough. What about the gym?

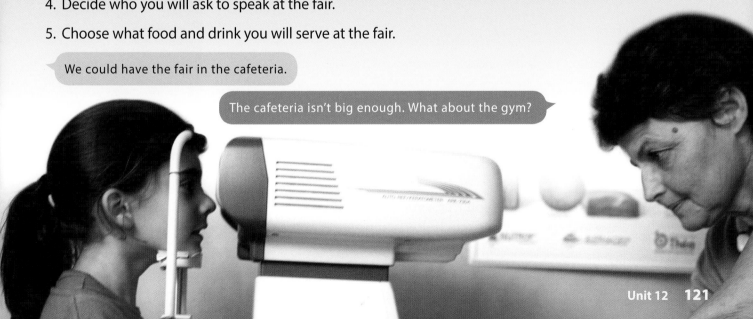

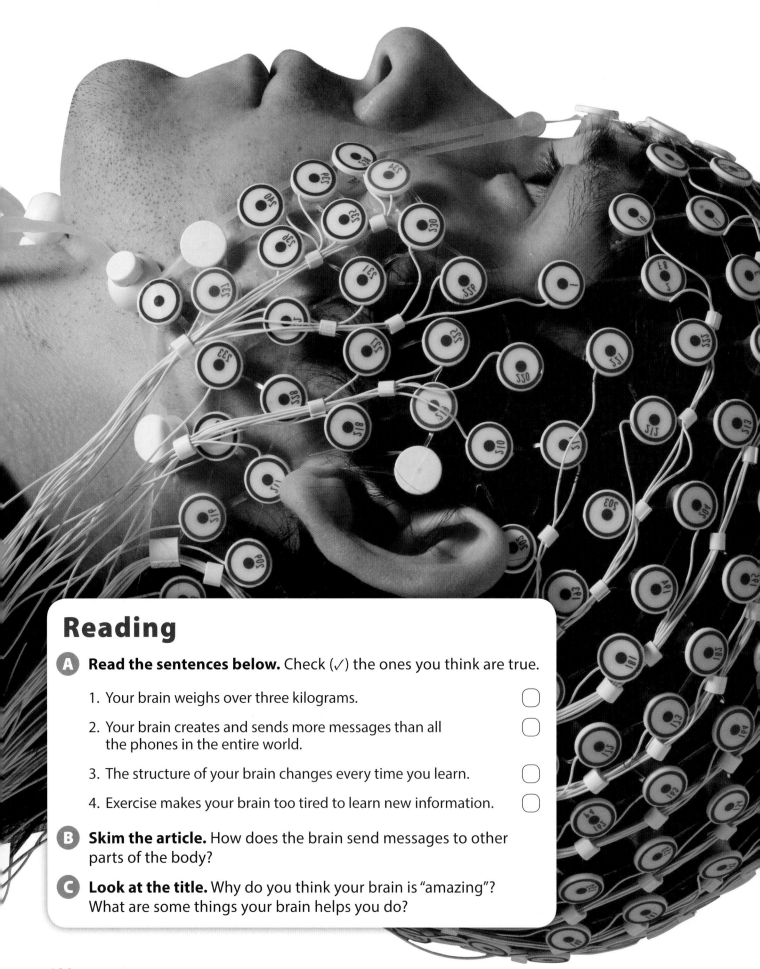

Reading

A **Read the sentences below.** Check (✓) the ones you think are true.

1. Your brain weighs over three kilograms. ⃝

2. Your brain creates and sends more messages than all the phones in the entire world. ⃝

3. The structure of your brain changes every time you learn. ⃝

4. Exercise makes your brain too tired to learn new information. ⃝

B **Skim the article.** How does the brain send messages to other parts of the body?

C **Look at the title.** Why do you think your brain is "amazing"? What are some things your brain helps you do?

YOUR AMAZING BRAIN

You carry a 1.3-kilogram mass of fatty material in your head that controls everything your body does. It lets you think, learn, create, and feel emotions. What's this amazing machine? It's your brain—a structure so incredible that the famous scientist James Watson called it "the most complex thing we
5 have yet discovered in our universe."

Your brain is faster and more powerful than a supercomputer.
Imagine that your cat jumps onto the kitchen counter, and is about to step onto a hot stove. In situations like this, your brain reads the signals from your eyes and quickly calculates when, where, and at what speed you need
10 to run to save her. Then it tells your muscles to move. No computer can match your brain's ability to download, process, and react to the flood of information from your eyes, ears, and other sensory organs.

Your brain generates enough electricity to turn on a light bulb.
Your brain contains about 100 billion tiny cells called neurons. Whenever you
15 dream, laugh, think, see, or move, tiny chemical and electrical signals are racing between these neurons along billions of tiny neural pathways. Countless messages fly around inside your brain every second, like a super-fast game of table tennis. Your neurons create and send more messages than all the phones in the entire world. And although a single neuron generates
20 only a tiny amount of electricity, all of them together can generate enough electricity to power a light bulb.

Neurons can send information to your brain extremely quickly.
If a bee lands on your foot, sensory neurons in your skin send this information to your brain at a speed of more than 240 kilometers per hour. Your brain
25 then uses motor neurons to send a message back to your foot: Shake the bee off quickly! Motor neurons can send this information at more than 320 kilometers per hour.

When you learn, you change the structure of your brain.
Riding a bike seems impossible at first, but you can soon master it. How? As
30 you practice, your brain sends "bike riding" messages along certain neural pathways again and again, forming new connections. In fact, the structure of your brain changes every time you learn, as well as whenever you have a new thought or memory.

Exercise helps make you smarter.
35 It is well known that exercise is great for your body and can even improve your mood. But scientists have also learned that your body produces a chemical after you exercise that makes it easier for your brain to learn. So, if you're stuck on a homework problem, go out and play soccer, and then try the problem again. You might discover that you're able to solve it!

A test recording the amount of electrical activity in the brain

Comprehension

A Answer the questions about *Your Amazing Brain*.

1. `Purpose` What is the purpose of the article?

   a. To describe how incredible the brain is

   b. To discuss the latest theories about the brain

   c. To show how little we know about the brain

2. `Vocabulary` In lines 11–12, "the flood of information" means _____ of information.

   a. a lack   b. a variety   c. a huge amount

3. `Detail` The processing power of your brain allows you to _____ in an emergency situation.

   a. react quickly   b. remain calm   c. be creative

4. `Detail` Each new memory or skill you gain creates new _____.

   a. motor neurons   b. sensory neurons   c. neural pathways

5. `Inference` If you were stuck on a homework problem, the author might suggest _____.

   a. playing tennis   b. taking a deep breath   c. doing a number puzzle

IDIOM

If someone wants to "pick your brain," they'll probably _____.

a. give you a brain scan
b. look at your test scores
c. ask you questions

B **Complete the summary.** Use the words in the box.

> signals   muscles   pathways   neurons   learn   brain

When you dream, laugh, think, or see, various (1) _____ race between (2) _____ along (3) _____. When your (4) _____ senses an emergency or needs your body to do something, it tells your (5) _____ to move. After you exercise, it is easier for your brain to (6) _____.

C **CRITICAL THINKING** **Talk with a partner.** Do you think there are differences between male and female brains? What do you think is different?

Writing

Write an action plan.
Set a health-related goal and create a step-by-step plan.

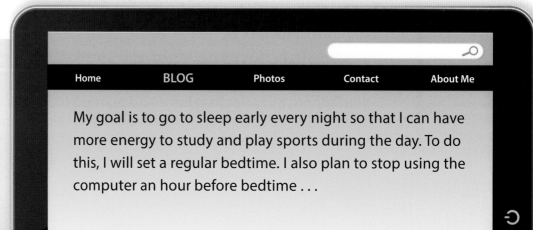

Home   BLOG   Photos   Contact   About Me

My goal is to go to sleep early every night so that I can have more energy to study and play sports during the day. To do this, I will set a regular bedtime. I also plan to stop using the computer an hour before bedtime . . .

Space Food

ABOUT THE VIDEO

Since the start of human space flight, NASA has been working to improve the food for its astronauts.

BEFORE YOU WATCH

Talk with a partner. What do you think are important features of space food? Circle the words in the box.

Space food has to be . . .

light	cheap	fresh	healthy
easy to hold	low in sugar	tasty	microwavable

WHILE YOU WATCH

A **Check your answers to the Before You Watch question.**

B **Watch the video again.** Circle the correct answers.

1. Freeze-dried food is (**lighter** / **heavier**) than regular food.

2. Freeze-dried food (**needs** / **doesn't need**) to be kept in a fridge.

3. Astronauts (**often** / **rarely**) eat fresh fruit.

4. In the video, the astronauts are having a special meal because it's (**Thanksgiving** / **Christmas**).

AFTER YOU WATCH

Talk with a partner. Do you think space food could be useful on Earth? If you went to space, what food would you want to take with you?

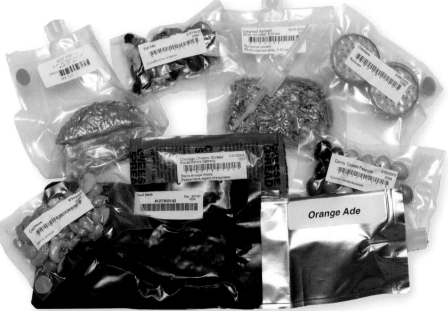

A meal in space

UNIT 3 LANGUAGE FOCUS

Work with a partner. Copy the words you wrote on page 29 in the spaces below. Then take turns reading each problem and giving each other advice.

Problem 1:

I want to dress better. My (1) _____ always gives me advice. He/She always says, "If I were you, I'd wear more colorful (2) _____ and (3) _____ . You'll look nicer." He/She also says (4) _____ is a good color for me. Should I take this advice? Do you have better advice for me?

Problem 2:

I want to have a healthier lifestyle. My sister says I should eat more (5) _____ and less (6) _____ . She says I could do more sports, like (7) _____ . Do you think this is good advice? What do you think I should do to have a healthier lifestyle?

UNIT 4 LANGUAGE FOCUS

Skim the news article. Ask your partner questions to complete the article. Use the words in parentheses to help you ask questions.

Student A:

A Cry for Help

A baby manatee calls out for her mother. She doesn't hear any reply. A man finds the baby and calls for help. He knows the baby won't survive without her mother—baby manatees need their mother to show them where to find food.

A rescue team rushes to the river. They see the baby manatee in the water. They lower a (1) _____ (**what**) into the water. They manage to catch the baby. They then carry her to the team's vehicle. Here, she is placed in a swimming pool and then driven to (2) _____ (**where**). The vet gives her (3) _____ (**what**). The examination shows that the baby, now named Kee, is underweight. To increase her weight, Kee is given milk (4) _____ (**how often**).

There is another manatee at the zoo, named Della. An accident with a boat caused her to be brought to the zoo. Della has given birth to a baby named Pal. This gives Virginia Edmonds, a caretaker at the zoo, an idea. She hopes Della will care for Kee like her baby. So the three manatees are placed in the same pool. Within hours, Della begins to feed Kee. Soon, they are doing everything together. They're one family now.

After five months, Della has recovered. It's time for her and her family to return to the wild. They are driven to the river's edge and released. "Kee is back where she belongs," says Edmonds.

UNIT 5 LANGUAGE FOCUS

Look at the photos below. Ask your partner questions about the Pancake Rocks.
Answer your partner's questions about The Valley of the Moon.

Student A:

The Valley of the Moon

The Pancake Rocks

What is The Valley of the Moon?

- The Valley of the Moon is a desert area in northwestern Argentina.

- The area has a dry and windy climate.

What's found there?

- Unusual rock formations—some are shaped like balls, others like towers, and even the Sphinx!

- Many dinosaur fossils are hidden within the rocks.

How were they formed?

- The rocks are up to 240 million years old. They were worn down by the wind.

- They were also shaped by rainwater.

What are the Pancake Rocks?

- The Pancake Rocks are _____ .

- The area also contains enormous _____ that shoot seawater high into the sky during high tides.

Where are they?

- The west coast of the South Island of New Zealand

How were they formed?

- They were formed over 30 million years ago from ancient _____ .

- The plants and animals were flattened by _____ , and formed limestone.

- The limestone has since been shaped by _____ , _____ , and _____ .

UNIT 4 LANGUAGE FOCUS

Skim the news article. Ask your partner questions to complete the article. Use the words in parentheses to help you ask questions.

Student B:

A Cry for Help

A baby manatee calls out for her mother. She doesn't hear any reply. A man finds the baby and calls for help. He knows the baby won't survive without her mother—baby manatees need their mother to show them where to find food.

A rescue team rushes to the river. They see the baby manatee in the water. They lower a small net into the water. They manage to catch the baby. They then carry her to the team's vehicle. Here, she is placed in a swimming pool and then driven to a local zoo. The vet gives her a checkup. The examination shows that the baby, now named Kee, is underweight. To increase her weight, Kee is given milk every three hours.

There is another manatee at the zoo, named Della. An accident with a
(5) _____ (**what**) caused her to be brought to the zoo. Della has given birth to a baby named Pal. This gives Virginia Edmonds, a caretaker at the zoo, an idea. She hopes Della will care for Kee like her baby. So the three manatees are placed in
(6) _____ (**where**). Within hours, Della begins to (7) _____
(**what**). Soon, they are doing everything together. They're one family now.

After five months, Della has recovered. It's time for her and her family to return to the wild. They are driven to the river's edge and (8) _____ (**what**). "Kee is back where she belongs," says Edmonds.

UNIT 11 COMMUNICATION

Read the information below.

Team A:

You **support** the project. Think of ways the building of the mall will benefit the town. Come up with a list of arguments. Think about these areas: the effect on the economy, jobs, and tourism. Also, think of points to counter Team B's possible arguments.

Follow these steps:

1. Team A: Present your arguments.

2. Team B: Counter Team A's arguments, and present your arguments.

3. Team A: Counter Team B's arguments, and summarize your arguments.

4. Team B: Summarize your arguments.

5. Discuss which team you think wins the debate.

UNIT 6 COMMUNICATION

Choose one of the animals below. Give clues using the facts provided. Don't say the name of the animal you've picked. If **Group B** guesses incorrectly, give another clue until they guess the animal. The team with the fewer guesses wins.

Group A:

Albatross (bird)

Life span in the wild: about 50 years

Habitat: Southern Ocean and North Pacific Ocean

Interesting fact 1: It drinks salt water.

Interesting fact 2: An albatross was once recorded circling the whole world in 46 days.

Interesting fact 3: It sometimes floats on the sea's surface.

Emperor penguin (bird)

Life span in the wild: 15 to 20 years

Habitat: Antarctica

Interesting fact 1: It can dive 565 m and stay underwater for more than 20 minutes.

Interesting fact 2: It only has one chick a year.

Interesting fact 3: It keeps the egg warm by covering it with feathered skin.

Bottlenose dolphin (mammal)

Life span in the wild: 45 to 50 years

Habitat: Warm and tropical waters around the world

Interesting fact 1: It can swim 30 km/h and jump almost 5 m out of the water.

Interesting fact 2: It only lets one half of its brain sleep at a time.

Interesting fact 3: It can use echolocation to find its prey.

Northern fur seal (mammal)

Life span in the wild: up to 26 years

Habitat: Cold waters of the north Pacific Ocean

Interesting fact 1: It usually looks for food at night.

Interesting fact 2: It has large eyes that let it see well underwater and at night.

Interesting fact 3: It has huge flippers to keep it cool.

Dugong (mammal)

Life span in the wild: about 70 years

Habitat: Warm coastal waters of the Red Sea, Indian Ocean, and Pacific Ocean

Interesting fact 1: It can stay underwater for 6 minutes.

Interesting fact 2: It is related to elephants.

Interesting fact 3: It was sometimes mistaken for a mermaid by sailors.

Hermit crab (shellfish)

Life span in the wild: up to 30 years

Habitat: Saltwater from shallow coastal areas to deep seas worldwide

Interesting fact 1: It is active at night.

Interesting fact 2: Some people keep them as pets.

Interesting fact 3: It often climbs over another of its kind instead of going around.

Group B's animals:

leatherback turtle	sea otter	manta ray
stonefish	saltwater crocodile	whale shark

UNIT 5 LANGUAGE FOCUS

Look at the photos below. Ask your partner questions about The Valley of the Moon. Answer your partner's questions about the Pancake Rocks.

Student B:

The Valley of the Moon

The Pancake Rocks

What is The Valley of the Moon?

- The Valley of the Moon is a _____ in northwestern Argentina.
- The area has a _____ climate.

What's found there?

- Unusual rock formations—some are shaped like _____, others like _____, and even the Sphinx!
- Many _____ fossils are hidden within the rocks.

How were they formed?

- The rocks are up to 240 million years old. They were worn down by _____.
- They were also shaped by _____.

What are the Pancake Rocks?

- The Pancake Rocks are layers of flat rock.
- The area also contains enormous "blowholes" that shoot seawater high into the sky during high tides.

Where are they?

- The west coast of the South Island of New Zealand

How were they formed?

- They were formed over 30 million years ago from ancient sea creatures and plants.
- The plants and animals were flattened by great water pressure, and formed limestone.
- The limestone has since been shaped by rain, wind, and seawater.

UNIT 6 COMMUNICATION

Choose one of the animals below. Give clues using the facts provided. Don't say the name of the animal you've picked. If **Group A** guesses incorrectly, give another clue until they guess the animal. The team with the fewer guesses wins.

Group B:

Leatherback turtle (reptile)
Life span in the wild: about 45 years

Habitat: Tropical and warm waters of the Atlantic, Pacific, and Indian Oceans, but seen in colder oceans, too

Interesting fact 1: It can dive 1,280 m and stay underwater for 85 minutes.

Interesting fact 2: It buries its eggs in the sand.

Interesting fact 3: It is endangered.

Sea otter (mammal)
Life span in the wild: up to 23 years

Habitat: Coasts of the Pacific Ocean in North America and Asia

Interesting fact 1: It washes itself in the ocean to keep clean after eating.

Interesting fact 2: It has to eat 3 hours a day to stay warm.

Interesting fact 3: It uses rocks to break open shellfish.

Manta ray (fish)
Life span in the wild: up to 20 years

Habitat: Warm waters, often near coral reefs

Interesting fact 1: It looks like a blanket.

Interesting fact 2: It looks dangerous but is actually very gentle.

Interesting fact 3: It eats about 13% of its body weight in food each week.

Stonefish (fish)
Life span in the wild: not known

Habitat: On coral reefs and near rocks, in warm and tropical waters of the Indian and Pacific Oceans

Interesting fact 1: It is one of the most poisonous fish in the world.

Interesting fact 2: It can live outside of the ocean for 20 hours.

Interesting fact 3: It hides itself and waits for its prey to swim past.

Saltwater crocodile (reptile)
Life span in the wild: up to 70 years

Habitat: Freshwater and saltwater areas of eastern India, southeast Asia, and northern Australia

Interesting fact 1: Some people say they are the animal most likely to eat a human.

Interesting fact 2: It kills 1–2 people every year in Australia.

Interesting fact 3: It sometimes swims far out to sea.

Whale shark (fish)
Life span in the wild: from 60 to 100 years

Habitat: Warm and tropical waters all over the world

Interesting fact 1: It looks dangerous but is actually very gentle.

Interesting fact 2: It eats tiny plants and animals.

Interesting fact 3: It can only reproduce when it is about 30 years old.

Group A's animals:

albatross   emperor penguin   bottlenose dolphin

northern fur seal   dugong   hermit crab

UNIT 11 COMMUNICATION

Read the information below.

Team B:

You **don't support** the project. Think of ways the building of the mall wouldn't be good for the town. Come up with a list of arguments. Think about these areas: the effect on small businesses, housing prices in areas near the mall, and the environment. Also, think of points to counter Team A's possible arguments.

Follow these steps:

1. Team A: Present your arguments.

2. Team B: Counter Team A's arguments, and present your arguments.

3. Team A: Counter Team B's arguments, and summarize your arguments.

4. Team B: Summarize your arguments.

5. Discuss which team you think wins the debate.

IRREGULAR PAST TENSE VERBS

BASE FORM	PAST FORM	PAST PARTICIPLE
become	became	become
bring	brought	brought
buy	bought	bought
catch	caught	caught
choose	chose	chosen
come	came	come
cost	cost	cost
cut	cut	cut
draw	drew	drawn
drink	drank	drunk
drive	drove	driven
eat	ate	eaten
fall	fell	fallen
feel	felt	felt
fight	fought	fought
find	found	found
fly	flew	flown
get	got	gotten
give	gave	given
go	went	gone
grow	grew	grown
hear	heard	heard
hurt	hurt	hurt
keep	kept	kept
know	knew	known
let	let	let
lose	lost	lost

BASE FORM	PAST FORM	PAST PARTICIPLE
make	made	made
mean	meant	meant
meet	met	met
pay	paid	paid
put	put	put
read	read	read
ride	rode	ridden
run	ran	run
say	said	said
see	saw	seen
sell	sold	sold
send	sent	sent
steal	stole	stolen
sing	sang	sung
sleep	slept	slept
speak	spoke	spoken
swim	swam	swum
take	took	taken
teach	taught	taught
tell	told	told
think	thought	thought
throw	threw	thrown
understand	understood	understood
wake	woke	woken
wear	wore	worn
win	won	won
write	wrote	written

LANGUAGE NOTES

UNIT 1 I LOVE MAKING JEWELRY!

VERB + -ING (STATEMENTS)

I You We They	**love** **like** **enjoy** **don't like** **hate** **can't stand**	**baking**. **doing puzzles**. **cooking**. **playing sports**.
He She	**loves** **likes** **enjoys** **doesn't like** **hates** **can't stand**	

VERB + -ING (QUESTIONS AND SHORT ANSWERS)

Do you Do they	**love** **like** **enjoy** **hate**	**baking**? **doing puzzles**?	Yes, I **do**. / No, I **don't**. Yes, they **do**. / No, they **don't**.
Does he Does she			Yes, he **does**. / No, he **doesn't**. Yes, she **does**. / No, she **doesn't**.

GERUNDS AS SUBJECTS

Skiing is great exercise.

Building models can be a lot of fun.

Performing in front of people makes me nervous.

UNIT 2 HOW LONG HAVE YOU BEEN PLAYING CRICKET?

PRESENT PERFECT PROGRESSIVE STATEMENTS (WITH *SINCE, FOR, LATELY, RECENTLY*)

I They	**have been playing** cricket **haven't been going** to the gym	**since** 2013. **for** a long time.
He She	**has been doing** archery **hasn't been playing** badminton	a lot **lately**. **recently**.

PRESENT PERFECT PROGRESSIVE (QUESTIONS)

How long **have** you **been working out**?

How long **has** he **been playing** rugby?

What **have** you **been doing since** breakfast?

What sports **has** he **been playing lately**?

What TV shows **have** they **been watching recently**?

Have you **been playing** the guitar **long**?

Has she **been doing** taekwondo **for** a long time?

Have they **been practicing** their dance **since** morning?

UNIT 3 YOU COULD ASK FOR ADVICE.

MODALS FOR ADVICE (QUESTIONS)

What	**should** **could**	I he she they	do to solve the problem?

MODALS FOR ADVICE (ANSWERS)

You He She They	**should** **could**	apologize. ask someone for help. try a different way of studying.
If I were you, I would		

TRY + GERUND

Have you **tried** **Why don't** you **try**	**saying** you're sorry? **talking** to a teacher? **explaining** your side of the story?

UNIT 4 THE KOALA WAS TAKEN TO A SHELTER.

ACTIVE VS. PASSIVE VOICE (1)

We use the active voice to say what the subject of the sentence does.

Subject	Active Verb	Object
Some people	**rescued**	the baby raccoon.
The vet	**attached**	three tracking tags.

ACTIVE VS. PASSIVE VOICE (2)

We use the passive voice when we want to change the object of the sentence into the subject.

Subject	Passive Verb
The baby raccoon	**was rescued**.
Three tracking tags	**were attached**.

PASSIVE VOICE

Simple Present	Simple Past
The koala **is wrapped** in a blanket.	The puppies **were checked** for injuries.
When **is** it **given** a bath?	What time **were** they **brought** in?
Is it **kept** in a cage overnight?	**Were** they **given** any medicine?

USE OF THE PASSIVE VOICE (1)

We use the passive voice if the subject is unknown or unimportant.

The pet cat **was abandoned** in a field.	(Someone or some people abandoned the cat, but it is unknown who did so.)
A baby bird **was brought** into the animal shelter.	(Someone or some people brought it in, but who did so is not important.)

USE OF THE PASSIVE VOICE (2)

We also use the passive voice to make general statements.

Kittens **are** usually **adopted** very quickly.

Wild animals **are** typically **checked** for any injuries.

UNIT 5 HOW WAS IT FORMED?

PASSIVE VOICE (WITH *BY*)

We use the passive voice to emphasize the receiver of an action. We use *by* to name the person or thing that does the action (the agent).

Present Progressive	Present Perfect
This beach **is being washed away by** the sea. **Why is** this park **being closed by** the Park Service? **Is** this glacier **being moved by** gravity?	The rock **has been broken apart by** freezing and melting ice. **How has** the Earth's environment **been changed by** pollution? **Has** this canyon **been shaped by** wind or water?

UNIT 6 LOOK AT THAT NARWHAL!

NON-RESTRICTIVE RELATIVE CLAUSES (*WHICH* AND *WHO*)

The seahorse, **which is a type of fish**, uses its tail to move forward.
Oceanography, **which is also called "marine science,"** is the scientific study of the world's oceans.
The Great Barrier Reef is an important habitat for millions of animals, **which depend on it for food and shelter**.

Tourists, **who don't always get proper training**, sometimes damage coral reefs.
Sylvia Earle, **who holds the world record for solo scuba diving**, is a National Geographic Explorer.
Jacques Cousteau, **who is probably the most famous oceanographer in the world**, died in 1997.

UNIT 7 IT MIGHT HAVE BEEN A TEMPLE.

MODALS OF PROBABILITY

	Less Sure	More Sure
Present	This stone **could**/**might** be worth a lot of money. It **might not** be an arrowhead.	This vase **can't**/**couldn't** be iron because it's too light. This **must** be the burial site. These coins don't have Latin on them, so they **must not** be Roman.
Past	Early traders **could**/**might** have left these gold coins here. They **might not** have built these statues by themselves.	This is made of gold. It **must** have belonged to someone important. They **couldn't** have left the island— they didn't have any boats.

UNIT 8 IT'S TALLER THAN THE EIFFEL TOWER!

TOO AND (NOT) ENOUGH

It's **too cloudy** today. I can't see anything.

You're **too old** to get the ticket discount. You need to be 18 or under.

He's **old enough** to drive. He just turned 16 so he has a license.

This car is **not big enough** for our family. We need a larger one.

(NOT) AS + ADJECTIVE + AS

I think living in Osaka is **as expensive as** Tokyo.

The Oakland Bay Bridge is probably **not as famous as** the Golden Gate Bridge.

COMPARATIVE AND SUPERLATIVE ADJECTIVES

Short adjectives (1 syllable)	fast deep	fast**er than** deep**er than**	**the** fast**est** **the** deep**est**
1-syllable adjectives (ending with a short vowel sound and a single consonant)	big hot	big**ger than** hot**ter than**	**the** big**gest** **the** hot**test**
Adjectives ending in -y	pretty hungry	prett**ier than** hungr**ier than**	**the** prett**iest** **the** hungr**iest**
Longer adjectives (2 or more syllables)	famous expensive	**more** famous **than** **more** expensive **than**	**the most** famous **the most** expensive
Irregular adjectives	good bad	**better than** **worse than**	**the best** **the worst**

UNIT 9 HE'S A GREAT DIRECTOR, ISN'T HE?

TAG QUESTIONS

Positive Statement + Negative Tag	Negative Statement + Positive Tag
It's a horror movie, **isn't it**?	It isn't a horror movie, **is it**?
They're famous, **aren't they**?	They aren't famous, **are they**?
She was watching a movie, **wasn't she**?	She wasn't watching a movie, **was she**?
They were popular, **weren't they**?	They weren't popular, **were they**?
He directs comedies, **doesn't he**?	He doesn't direct comedies, **does he**?
They appear in action movies, **don't they**?	They don't appear in action movies, **do they**?
You liked that movie, **didn't you**?	You didn't like that movie, **did you**?
We've seen *Star Wars*, **haven't we**?	We haven't seen *Star Wars*, **have we**?
I can watch that movie, **can't I**?	I can't watch that movie, **can I**?
She should buy a ticket, **shouldn't she**?	She shouldn't buy a ticket, **should she**?
They'll win an award, **won't they**?	They won't win an award, **will they**?

TAG QUESTIONS (IRREGULAR FORMS)

I'm invited, **aren't I**?	I'm not invited, **am I**?
You **have to** be 21 to enter, **don't** you?	You **don't have to** be 21 to enter, **do** you?

TAG QUESTIONS (SHORT ANSWERS)

George Lucas directed *Star Wars*, **didn't he**? George Lucas didn't direct *Star Wars*, **did he**?	**Yes, he did** (He did direct it.)
Steven Spielberg directed *Star Wars*, **didn't he**? Steven Spielberg didn't direct *Star Wars*, **did he**?	**No, he didn't**. (He did not direct it.)

UNIT 10 I WISH I COULD BE AN ATHLETE!

WISH

I am not young.	I **wish** I **were** young.
I don't have a job.	I **wish** I **had** a job.
I have a test tomorrow.	I **wish** I **didn't have** a test tomorrow.
I can't fly.	I **wish** I **could fly**.

SECOND CONDITIONAL (STATEMENTS)

If I **had** a lot of money, I**'d travel** around the world.

If I **didn't have** a test tomorrow, I**'d go** watch a movie.

If I **could choose** any superpower, I**'d want** to be able to read people's minds.

SECOND CONDITIONAL (QUESTIONS AND SHORT ANSWERS)

If you **didn't have** to go to school, **would** you **go** anyway?	Yes, I **would**. /
If you **could travel** back in time, **would** you **want** to?	No, I **wouldn't**.

UNIT 11 WHAT WOULD YOU DO?

PRESENT PERFECT PROGRESSIVE

Someone **has been borrowing** my things without asking.

My neighbors **have been having** loud parties lately.

PASSIVE VOICE

Small animals **are** often **adopted** very quickly.

The injured bear **was given** medicine to calm it down.

The injured dog **is being treated** right now.

The adult turtles **have been released** into the sea.

The animal rescue league **is supported by** hundreds of volunteers.

Several trees in the park **were cut down by** illegal loggers.

The face of the statue **has been eroded away by** the wind.

GIVING ADVICE

You **could** apologize.

You **should** find out the cause of the problem.

Have you **tried asking** for help?

Why don't you talk to your family about it?

MODALS OF PROBABILITY

This coin **could**/**might** be iron.

This **might not** be gold.

The royal family **could**/**might** have escaped from the city.

The ship's captain **might not** have realized his mistake in time.

This bag **can't**/**couldn't** be Diana's. She didn't bring one today.

This **must** be the king's tomb. Look at all the gold!

The city **must** have been very beautiful back then. Look at these drawings!

They **couldn't** have made these tools. They didn't know how to work with iron.

SECOND CONDITIONAL

If I **had** more time, I**'d take** a night class.

If I **didn't have** a class at 4:00, I**'d play** basketball.

If I **could cure** any disease, I**'d want** to cure cancer.

UNIT 12 YOU SHOULD EAT MORE FRUIT!

GERUNDS

I love **working out**.

I don't like **eating** a lot of red meat.

Exercising helps reduce stress.

COMPARATIVE AND SUPERLATIVE ADJECTIVES

Juice is **healthier than** soda.

Fresh fruit is **more expensive than** canned fruit.

Whole grain bread is **better** for you **than** white bread.

TOO AND (NOT) ENOUGH

I'm **too tired** to continue running.

Talia is **tall enough** to take the roller coaster.

Alex is **not strong enough** to lift that desk.

(NOT) AS + ADJECTIVE + AS

Vegetable burgers are **just as tasty as** beef burgers.

Turkey is **not as fatty as** lamb.

NON-RESTRICTIVE RELATIVE CLAUSES

Fast food, **which** is often high in calories, is junk food.

My cousin, **who** studied sports science in college, is now a personal trainer.

TAG QUESTIONS

Avocados are good for you, **aren't they**?

Paul went to the farmers' market, **didn't he**?

Todd and Allison won't be at the race, **will they**?

Iris isn't going to the supermarket, **is she**?

Photo Credits

1 Massimo Borchi/Atlantide Phototravel/Corbis, **3** mbbirdy/Getty Images, **4–5** Cristian Zamfir/Shutterstock, **6–7 13** Howard Grey/Ocean/Corbis, **9** Hero Images/Corbis, **10** National Geographic Channel, **11** heshphoto/Image Source/Corbis, **15** ails.arc.nasa.gov, **16–17** Felix Hug/Terra/Corbis, **19** Hero Images/Getty Images, **20** Gonzalo Fuentes/Reuters, **21** (t) Alberto Pizzolig/AFP/Getty Images, (b) J and J Productions/Getty Images, **22–23** Bryan Hansel, **24** (b) Lucy Nicholson/Reuters, **25** (c) www.liferollson.org, (b) Venice Beach Photos, **26–27** Matt McClain/The Washington Post/Getty Images, **29** Chris Schmidt/Getty Images, **30** Linda Makarov/NGC, **31** (t) Tupungato/Shutterstock, (b) Jamie Kingham/Image Source/Corbis, **32–33** Christopher Drost/Corbis Wire/Corbis, **35** Mark Thiessen/NGC, **36–37** Joel Sartore/NGC, **39** Robert Galbraith/Reuters, **40** Joel Sartore/NGC, **41** Brian J. Skerry/National Geographic/Getty Images, **42–43** Town of Truckee Animal Services, **44** Carrie Vonderhaar/Ocean Futures Society/NGC, **45** Joel Sartore/NGC, **46–47** Nigel Killeen/Getty Images, **46** (b) Win Huang/Shutterstock, **49** Louie Psihoyos/Terra/Corbis, **50** Arctic-Images/Encyclopedia/Corbis, **51** (t) Artography/Shutterstock, **52–53** Ryan Deboodt, **54** Pablo Rogat/Shutterstock, **55** Ryan Deboodt, **56–57** Paul Nicklen/NGC, **59** NGC, **60** (t) Cb2/Zob/Wenn.com/Newscom, (br) Robert Clark/NGC, **61** (t) Gouraud Studio/Shutterstock, (b) Robert Haasmann/Alloy/Corbis, **62** (bg) David Doubilet/Getty Images, (b) NGC, **65** David Doubilet/National Geographic/Getty Images, **66–67** www.tonnaja.com/Getty Images, **69** NGC, **70** NGC, **71** (t) Bridgeman Art Library/Getty Images, (c) Sergej Razvodovskij/Shutterstock, (b) Fer Gregory/Shutterstock, **72–73** Michel Gounot/Godong/Terra/Corbis, **75** Jaroslav Moravcik/Shutterstock, **76–77** Fayez Nureldine/AFP/Getty Images, **77** Image Source/Corbis, **79** Kenneth Garrett/NGC, **80** BNKR Arquitectura/Solent, **81** Henryk Sadura/Shutterstock, **82–83** Seaorbiter – Jacques Rougerie, **84** AP Images/Imaginechina/Liu jianmin, **85** Jason Andrew/Getty Images, **86–87** Arnaldo Magnani/Getty Images, **89** flas100/Shutterstock, **90** Photos 12/Alamy, **91** (t) Africa Studio/Shutterstock, (b) Vertes Edmond Mihai/Shutterstock, **92–93** Patrick Foto/Shutterstock, **95** Jtb Media Creation, Inc./Alamy, **96–97** Lars Baron/Bongarts/Getty Images, **99** Jetta Productions/Walter Hodges/Getty Images, **100** Joel Sartore/NGC, **101** (t) TTstudio/Shutterstock, **102–103** (bg) Raphael Dias/Rede Globo, **102** (t) Paula Aguilera/MIT Media Lab, **105** NGC, **106–107** Ammentorp Photography/Shutterstock, **109** RubberBall/Alamy, **110** Milk Photographie/Cardinal/Corbis, **111** (t) Cliparea L Custom Media/Shutterstock, (b) Dado Galdieri/Bloomberg/Getty Images, **112–113** Comstock/Getty Images, **115** (c) 1996–2015 National Geographic Channel, (b) mrkornflakes/Shutterstock, **116–117** Celin Serbo/Aurora Photos, **119** William Sallaz/Flame/Corbis, **120** Michael Pole/Flame/Corbis, **121** (t) Robyn Mackenzie/Shutterstock, (b) BSIP/UIG/Getty Images, **122–123** Maggie Steber/NGC, **125** NASA, **127, 130** (tl) Photograph by Michael Schwab/Getty Images, (tr) Marco Simoni/cultura/Corbis

NGC = National Geographic Creative

Art Credits

7 (tl) Kozyrina Olga/Shutterstock, (tl) Sureewan Pengtip/Shutterstock, (tr) Bioraven/Shutterstock, (tr) cheesekerbs/Shutterstock, **8, 18, 28, 38, 48, 58, 68, 78, 88, 98, 108, 118** Raketshop, **17** (tl) Leremy/Shutterstock, (tl) Mushakesa/Shutterstock, (tr) snorks/Shutterstock, (tr) Mushakesa/Shutterstock, **22** Lachina

Acknowledgments

The authors and publisher would like to thank the following individuals and organizations who offered many helpful insights, ideas, and suggestions during the development of **Time Zones**.

Asia and Europe

Phil Woodall, Aoyama Gakuin Senior High School; **Suzette Buxmann**, Aston A+; **Wayne Fong**, Aston English; Berlitz China; Berlitz Germany; Berlitz Hong Kong; Berlitz Japan; Berlitz Singapore; **Anothai Jetsadu**, Cha-am Khunying Nuangburi School; **Rui-Hua Hsu**, Chi Yong High School; **Gary Darnell**, DEU Private School, Izmir; **Hwang Soon Hee, Irean Yeon, Junhee Im, Seungeun Jung**, Eun Seok Elementary School; **Hyun Ah Park**, Gachon University; **Hsi-Tzu Hung**, Hwa Hsia Institute of Technology; **Kate Sato**, Kitopia English School; **Daniel Stewart**, Kaisei Junior and Senior High School; **Haruko Morimoto, Ken Ip**, Mejiro Kenshin Junior and Senior High School; **Sovoan Sem**, Milky Way School; **Shu-Yi Chang**, Ming Dao High School; **Ludwig Tan**, National Institute of Education; **Tao Rui, Yuan Wei Hua**, New Oriental Education & Technology Group; **Tom Fast**, Okayama Gakugeikan High School; **Yu-Ping Luo**, Oriental Institute of Technology; **Jutamas**, Prakhanong Pittayalai School; **Akira Yasuhara**, Rikkyo Ikebukuro Junior and Senior High School; **Matthew Rhoda**, Sakuragaoka Junior and Senior High School; **Michael Raship, Nicholas Canales**, Scientific Education Group Co; **Andrew O'Brien**, Second Kyoritsu Girls Junior and Senior High School; **Atsuko Okada**, Shinagawa Joshi Gakuin Junior and Senior High School; **Sheila Yu**, Shin Min High School; **Stewart Dorward**, Shumei Junior and Senior High School; **Gaenor Hardy**, Star English Centres; **Philip Chandler, Thomas Campagna**, Tama University Meguro Junior and Senior High School; **Lois Wang**, Teachall English; **Iwao Arai, James Daly, Satomi Kishi**, Tokyo City University Junior and Senior High School; **Jason May**, Tokyo Seitoku University High School; **Amnoui Jaimipak**, Triamudomsuksapattanakarn Chiangrai School; **Jonee de Leon**, Universal English Center; **Thiwaphorn Tharawatcharasart**, Uthaiwitthayakhom School; **Richard Ascough**, Wayo Women's University; **Kirvin Andrew Dyer**, Yan Ping High School

The Americas

Allynne Fraemam, Flávia Carneiro, Jonathan Reinaux, Mônica Carvalho, ABA; **Antonio Fernando Pinho**, Academia De Idiomas; **Wilmer Escobar**, Academia Militar; **Adriana Rupp, Denise Silva, Jorge Mendes**, ACBEU; **Rebecca Gonzalez**, AIF Systems English Language Institute; **Camila Vidal Suárez, Adriana Yaffe, Andrea da Silva, Bruno Oliveri, Diego A. Fábregas Acosta, Fabiana Hernandez, Florencia Barrios, Ignacio Silveira Trabal, Lucía Greco Castro, Lucy Pintos, Silvia Laborde**, Alianza Cultural Uruguay Estados Unidos; **Adriana Alvarez**, ASICANA; **Corina C. Machado Correa, Silvia Helena R. D. Corrêa, Mariana M. Paglione Vedana**, Associacao Alumni; Berlitz, Colombia; Berlitz Mexico; Berlitz Peru; Berlitz US; **Simone Ashton**, Britanic Madalena; **Keith Astle**, Britanic Piedade; **Dulce Capiberibe**, Britanic Setúbal; **Matthew Gerard O'Conner**, Britanic Setúbal; **Viviane Remígio**, Britanic Setúbal; **Adriana da Silva, Ana Raquel F. F. Campos, Ebenezer Macario, Giselle Schimaichel, Larissa Platinetti, Miriam Alves Carnieletto, Selma Oliveira**, Centro Cultural Brasil Estados Unidos CCBEU; **Amiris Helena**, CCDA; **Alexandra Nancy Lake Sawada, Ana Tereza R. P. Moreira, Denise Helena Monteiro, Larissa Ferreria, Patricia Mckay Aronis**, CELLEP; **Claudia Patricia Gutierrez, Edna Zapata, Leslie Cortés, Silvia Elena Martinez, Yesid Londoño**, Centro Colombo Americano-Medellin; **Gabriel Villamar Then**, Centro Educativo los Prados; **Monica Lugo**, Centro Escolar Versalles; **Adriane Caldas, Simone Raupp, Sylvia Formoso**, Colégio Anchieta; **José Olavo de Amorim**, Colégio Bandeirantes; **Dionisio Alfredo Meza Solar**, Colegio Cultural I; **Madson Gois Diniz**, Colegio De Aplicação; **Ilonka Diaz, Melenie Gonzalez**, Colegio Dominico Espanol; **Laura Monica Cadena, Rebeca Perez**, Colegio Franco Ingles; **Jedinson Trujillo**, Colegio Guías; **Christophe Flaz, Isauro Sanchez Gutierrez**, Colegio Iglesa Bautista Fundamenta; **Ayrton Lambert**, Colégio Il Peretz; **Samuel Jean Baptiste**, Colegio Instituto Montessori; **Beatriz Galvez, Evelyn Melendez**, Colegio Los Olivos; **Carlos Gomez, Diana Herrera Ramirez, Diana Pedraza Aguirre, Karol Bibana Hutado Morales**, Colegio Santa Luisa; **Marta Segui Rivas**, Colegio Velmont; **Thays Ladosky**, DAMAS; **Amalia Vasquez, Ana Palencia, Fernando de Leon, Isabel Cubilla, Leonel Zapata, Lorena Chavarria, Maria Adames**, English Access Microscholarship Program; **Rosângela Duarte Dos Santos**, English Space; **Walter Junior Ribeiro Silva**, Friends Language Center; **Luis Reynaldo Frias**, Harvard Institute; **Carlos Olavo Queiroz Guimarães, Elisa Borges, Patricia Martins, Lilian Bluvol Vaisman, Samara Camilo Tomé Costa**, IBEU; **Gustavo Sardo, João Carlos Queiroz Furtado, Rafael Bastos, Vanessa Rangel**, IBLE; **Graciela Martin**, ICANA (BELGRANO); **Carlos Santanna, Elizabeth Gonçalves**, ICBEU; **Inês Greve Milke, João Alfredo Bergmann**, Instituto Cultural Brasileiro Norte-Americano; **Tarsis Perez**, ICDA-Instituto Cultural Dominico Americano; **Cynthia Marquez, Guillermo Cortez, Ivan Quinteros, Luis Morales R, Melissa Lopez, Patricia Perez, Rebeca de Arrue, Rebeca Martinez de Arrue**, Instituto Guatemalteco Americano; **Renata Lucia Cardoso**, Instituto Natural de Desenvolvimento Infantil; **Graciela Nobile**, Instituto San Diego; **Walter Guevara**, Pio XII; **Juan Omar Valdez**, Professional Training Systems; **Carlos Carmona, Eugenio Altieri, Regan Albertson**, Progressive English Services; **Raul Billini**, Prolingua; **Juan Manuel Marin, Luisa Fecuanda Infort, Maria Consuelo Arauijo**, Providencia; **Carmen Gehrke**, Quatrum, Porto Alegre; **Rodrigo Rezende**, Seven; **Lcuciano Joel del Rosario**, St. José School; **Sabino Morla**, UASD; **Silvia Regina D'Andrea**, União Cultural Brasil-Estados Unidos; **Ruth Salomon-Barkemeyer**, Unilínguas Sao Leopoldo; **Anatalia Souza, Livia Rebelo**, UNIME-Ingles Para Criancas-Salvador; **Andrei dos Santos Cunha, Brigitte Mund, Gislaine Deckmann, Jeane Blume Cortezia, Rosana Gusmão**, Unisinos; **Diego Pérez**, Universidad de Ibague; **Beatriz Daldosso Felippe**, U.S. Idiomas Universe School

David Bohlke would like to thank the entire editorial team at National Geographic Learning for their dedication to producing such stimulating and engaging learning materials. He would also like to thank Jennifer Wilkin and the rest of the *Time Zones* author team for making the first edition such a success.